divine desserts

divine desserts

SENSATIONAL RECIPES FOR DELECTABLE DISHES

CONTRIBUTING EDITOR:
ROSEMARY WILKINSON

LORENZ BOOKS

First published by Lorenz Books in 2001

© Anness Publishing Limited 2001

Lorenz Books is an imprint of Anness Publishing Limited
Hermes House, 88–89 Blackfriars Road, London SE1 8HA

Published in the USA by Lorenz Books, Anness Publishing Inc.
27 West 20th Street, New York, NY 10011

www.lorenzbooks.com

This edition distributed in Canada by Raincoast Books
9050 Shaughnessy Street, Vancouver, British Columbia V6P 6E5

All rights reserved. No part of this publication may be reproduced, stored in a retrieval system, or transmitted in any way or by any means, electronic, mechanical, photocopying, recording or otherwise, without the prior written permission of the copyright holder.

A CIP catalogue record for this book is available from the British Library.

Publisher: Joanna Lorenz
Copy Editor: Karen Douthwaite
Designer: Bill Mason
Recipes: Carla Capalbo, Francis Cleary, Deh-Ta Hsiung, Norma MacMillan,
Laura Washburn and Stephen Wheeler
Photographers: Karl Adamson, Edward Allwright, Steve Baxter, James Duncan,
Amanda Heywood, Don Last and Michael Michaels
Food for Photography: Carla Capalbo, Francis Cleary, Carole Handslip, Jane Hartshorn,
Wendy Lee, Jane Stevenson and Elizabeth Wolf Cohen
Stylists: Carla Capalbo, Madeleine Brehaut, Diana Civil, Amanda Heywood,
Maria Kelly, Blake Minton, Kirsty Rawlings and Fiona Tillett
Front cover: William Lingwood, Photographer; Helen Trent, Stylist; Sunil Vijayakar, Food Stylist

Previously published as part of a larger compendium, *Best Ever Desserts*

1 3 5 7 9 10 8 6 4 2

NOTES
Bracketed terms are intended for American readers.

For all recipes, quantities are given in both metric and imperial measures and, where appropriate, measures are also given in standard cups and spoons. Follow one set, but not a mixture, because they are not interchangeable.

Standard spoon and cup measures are level.
1 tsp = 5ml, 1 tbsp = 15ml, 1 cup = 250ml/8fl oz

Australian standard tablespoons are 20ml. Australian readers should use 3 tsp in place of 1 tbsp for measuring small quantities of gelatine, flour, salt, etc.

Medium (US large) eggs are used unless otherwise stated.

Contents

Introduction
6

Cold Desserts
16

Hot Puddings
38

Quick and Easy
56

Low Calorie
66

Cakes and Gâteaux
74

Tarts and Pies
84

Index
96

Introduction

Desserts are all about self-indulgence. In today's stress-filled world, the pleasure to be gained from preparing and sharing a delicious sweet dish, whether elegant and sophisticated or evocative of childhood nostalgia, is a thing to be treasured. Even those who are concerned about their calorie intake need not miss out – there is a selection of healthy dishes here which need not induce guilt.

This book presents a wealth of enticing recipes ranging from the lightest soufflé to the richest chocolate pudding. With so much choice, you are sure to find the perfect dessert for every occasion, whether a light, refreshing dish to be served after a filling main course, or a rich, creamy dessert to follow a less substantial dish. There are fabulous gâteaux, classic baked custards, a wicked trifle, irresistible fruity tarts, pies and cheesecakes, chocolate desserts of every kind, and warm and comforting crumbles. For those short on time, there is a range of quick and easy

Left: *A mouth-watering variation of the classic Italian dessert,* Hot Chocolate Zabaglione *(page 40).*

Right: *The combination of soft fruit and creamy white chocolate is simply irresistible in this traditionally baked* Raspberry and White Chocolate Cheesecake *(page 23).*

dishes that are as tasty as they are speedy to create. Many of the recipes can be partly or completely prepared in advance, which makes them the perfect choice for entertaining, enabling you to relax and enjoy the meal as much as your guests.

All the recipes have clear step-by-step instructions, and you will find that even the traditionally tricky soufflés and roulades are easy to make and will look and taste absolutely delicious. In this comprehensive introductory section you'll find basic recipes for classic pastries and sauces, including cook's techniques for pastry-making and handling. Throughout the book there are plenty of helpful hints, tips, and variations for using alternative ingredients to ring the changes.

With chapters on cold desserts, hot puddings, quick and easy desserts, low calorie desserts and more, there is something here for everyone. So read on and enjoy creating the most divine desserts – for anytime and every occasion.

Making Shortcrust (Pie Crust) Pastry

A meltingly crisp, crumbly pastry sets off any filling to perfection, whether sweet or savoury. The fat content of the pastry dough can be made up of half butter or margarine and half white vegetable fat, or can be all one kind of fat.

INGREDIENTS

For a 23cm/9in pastry case
225g/8oz/2 cups plain (all-purpose) flour
1.5ml/¼ tsp salt
115g/4oz/8 tbsp fat, chilled and diced

1 Sift the flour and salt into a bowl. Add the fat. Rub it into the flour with your fingertips until the mixture is crumbly.

2 Sprinkle 45ml/3 tbsp of iced water over the mixture. With a fork, toss gently to mix and moisten it.

3 Press the dough into a ball. If it is too dry to hold together, gradually add another 15ml/1 tbsp of iced water.

4 Wrap the ball of dough with clear film (plastic wrap) or greaseproof paper and chill for at least 30 minutes.

5 To make pastry in a food processor: combine the flour, salt and cubed fat in the work bowl. Process, turning the machine on and off, just until the mixture is crumbly. Add 45–60ml/3–4 tbsp of iced water and process again briefly – just until the dough starts to pull away from the sides of the bowl. It should still look crumbly. Remove the dough from the processor and gather it into a ball. Wrap and chill.

SHORTCRUST PASTRY VARIATIONS

For Nut Shortcrust
Add 30g/1oz/¼ cup finely chopped walnuts or pecan nuts to the flour mixture.

For Rich Shortcrust
Use 225g/8oz/2 cups flour and 175g/6oz/¾ cup fat (preferably all butter), plus 15ml/1 tbsp caster (superfine) sugar if making a sweet pie. Bind with 1 egg yolk and 30–45ml/2–3 tbsp water.

For a Two-crust Pie
Increase the proportions for these pastries by 50%, thus the amounts needed for basic shortcrust pastry are: 340g/12oz/3 cups flour, 2.5ml/½ tsp salt, 175g/6oz/¾ cup fat, 75–90ml/5–6 tbsp water.

PASTRY MAKING TIPS

It helps if the fat is cold and firm, particularly if making the dough in a food processor. Cold fat has less chance of warming and softening too much when it is being rubbed into the flour, resulting in an oily pastry. Use block margarine rather than the soft tub-type (whipped type) for the same reason.

When rubbing the fat into the flour, if it begins to soften and feel oily, put the bowl in the refrigerator to chill for 20–30 minutes. Then continue to make the dough.

Liquids used should be ice-cold so that they will not soften or melt the fat.

Take care when adding the water: start with the smaller amount (added all at once, not in a dribble), and add more only if the mixture will not come together into a dough. Too much water will make the dough difficult to handle and will result in tough pastry.

When gathering the mixture together into a ball of dough, handle it as little as possible: overworked dough will again produce a tough pastry.

To avoid shrinkage, chill the pastry dough before rolling out and baking. This 'resting time' will allow any elasticity developed during mixing to relax.

Making French Flan Pastry

The pastry for tarts and flans is made with butter or margarine, giving a rich and crumbly result. The more fat used, the richer the pastry will be, and the harder to roll out. If you have difficulty rolling it, you can press it into the tin instead, or roll it out between sheets of clear film (plastic wrap). Flan pastry, like shortcrust, can be made by hand or in a food processor. Tips for making, handling and using shortcrust pastry apply equally to this type of pastry.

INGREDIENTS

For a 23cm/9in flan case

200g/7oz/1¾ cups plain (all-purpose) flour
2.5ml/½ tsp salt
115g/4oz/½ cup butter or margarine, chilled
1 egg yolk
1.5ml/¼ tsp lemon juice

1 Sift the flour and salt into a bowl. Add the butter or margarine. Rub into the flour until the mixture resembles fine breadcrumbs.

2 In a small bowl, mix the egg yolk, lemon juice and 30ml/2 tbsp of iced water. Add to the flour mixture. With a fork, toss gently to mix and moisten.

3 Press the dough into a rough ball. If it is too dry to come together, add 15ml/1 tbsp more water. Turn on to the work surface or a pastry board.

4 With the heel of your hand, push small portions of dough away from you, smearing them on the surface.

5 Continue mixing the dough in this way until it feels pliable and can be peeled easily off the work surface or pastry board.

6 Press the dough into a smooth ball. Wrap in clear film (plastic wrap) and chill for at least 30 minutes.

FLAN PASTRY VARIATIONS

For Sweet Flan Pastry
Reduce the amount of salt to 1.5ml/¼ tsp, add 15ml/1 tbsp caster (superfine) sugar with the flour.

For Rich Flan Pastry
Use 200g/7oz/1¾ cups flour, 2.5ml/½ tsp salt, 150g/5oz/10 tbsp butter, 2 egg yolks, and 15–30ml/1–2 tbsp water.

For Rich Sweet Flan Pastry
Make rich flan pastry, adding 45ml/3 tbsp caster sugar with the flour and, if liked, 2.5ml/½ tsp vanilla essence (extract) with the egg yolks.

Making Choux Pastry

Unlike other pastries, where the fat is rubbed into the flour, with choux pastry the butter is melted with water and then the flour is added, followed by eggs. The result is more of a paste than a dough. It is easy to make, but care must be taken in measuring the ingredients.

INGREDIENTS

For 18 profiteroles or 12 éclairs

115g/4oz/½ cup butter, cut into small pieces
10ml/2 tsp caster (superfine) sugar (optional)
1.5ml/¼ tsp salt
150g/5oz/1¼ cups plain (all-purpose) flour
4 eggs, beaten to mix
1 egg, beaten with 5ml/1 tsp cold water, for glaze

1 Preheat the oven to 220°C/425°F/Gas 7. Combine the butter, sugar, if using, salt and 250ml/8fl oz/1 cup of water in a large heavy pan. Bring to the boil over a moderately high heat, stirring occasionally.

2 As soon as the mixture is boiling, remove the pan from the heat. Add the flour all at once and beat vigorously with a wooden spoon to mix the flour smoothly into the liquid.

3 Return the pan to moderate heat and cook, stirring, until the mixture forms a ball, pulling away from the side of the pan. This will take about 1 minute. Remove from the heat again and allow to cool for 3–5 minutes.

4 Add a little of the beaten eggs and beat well to incorporate. Add a little more egg and beat in well. Continue beating in the eggs until the mixture becomes a smooth and shiny paste.

5 While still warm, shape choux puffs, éclairs, profiteroles or rings on a baking sheet lined with baking parchment.

6 Glaze with 1 egg beaten with 5ml/1tsp of cold water. Put into the preheated oven, then reduce the heat to 200°C/400°F/Gas 6. Bake until puffed and golden brown.

SHAPING CHOUX PASTRY

For Large Puffs
Use two large spoons dipped in water. Drop the paste in 5–6cm/2–2½in wide blobs on the paper-lined baking sheet, leaving 4cm/1½in between each. Neaten the blobs as much as possible. Alternatively, for well-shaped puffs, pipe the paste using a piping (pastry) bag fitted with a 2cm/¾in plain nozzle.

For Profiteroles
Use a tablespoon, two small spoons or a piping bag fitted with a 1cm/½in nozzle and shape 2.5cm/1in blobs.

For Eclairs
Use a piping bag fitted with a 2cm/¾in nozzle. Pipe strips 10–13cm/4–5in long.

For a Ring
Draw a 30cm/12in circle on the paper. Spoon the paste in large blobs on the circle to make a ring. Or pipe two rings around the circle and a third on top.

BAKING TIMES FOR CHOUX PASTRY

Large puffs and éclairs	30–35 minutes
Profiteroles	20–25 minutes
Rings	40–45 minutes

Rolling Out Pastry and Lining a Pie Tin

A neat pastry case that doesn't distort or shrink in baking is the desired result. The key to success is handling the dough gently. Use the method here to line a round pie or tart tin that is about 5cm/2in deep.

Remove the chilled dough from the refrigerator and allow it to soften slightly at room temperature. Unwrap and put it on a lightly floured surface. Flatten the dough into a neat, round disc. Lightly flour the rolling pin.

1. Using even pressure, start rolling out the dough, working from the centre to the edge each time and easing the pressure slightly as you reach the edge.

2. Lift up the dough and give it a quarter turn from time to time during the rolling. This will prevent the dough sticking to the surface, and will help keep the thickness even.

3. Continue rolling out until the dough circle is about 5cm/2in larger all round than the tin. It should be about 3mm/⅛in thick.

4. Set the rolling pin on the dough, near one side of the circle. Fold the outside edge of the dough over the pin, then roll the pin over the dough to wrap the dough round it. Do this gently and loosely.

5. Hold the pin over the tin and gently unroll the dough so it drapes into the tin, centring it as much as possible.

6. With your fingertips, lift and ease the dough into the tin, gently pressing it over the bottom and up the side. Turn excess dough over the rim and trim it with a knife or scissors, depending on the edge to be made.

Finishing the Edge

1. *For a forked edge:* trim the dough even with the rim and neaten it. Firmly and evenly press the prongs of a fork all round the edge. If the fork sticks, dip it in flour every so often.

2. *For a crimped edge:* trim the dough to leave an overhang of about 1.5cm/½in all round. Fold the extra dough under. Put the knuckle or tip of the index finger of one of your hands inside the edge, pointing directly out. With the thumb and index finger of your other hand, pinch the dough edge around your index finger into a "V" shape. Continue all the way round the edge.

3. *For a ruffled edge:* trim the dough to leave an overhang of about 1.5cm/½in all round. Fold the extra dough under. Hold the thumb and index finger of one of your hands about 2.5cm/1in apart, inside the edge, pointing directly out. With the index finger of your other hand, gently pull the dough between them, to the end of the rim. Continue this all the way round the edge.

4. *For a cutout edge:* trim the dough even with the rim and press it flat on the rim. With a small fancy cutter, cut out decorative shapes from the dough trimmings. Moisten the edge of the pastry case and press the cutouts in place, overlapping them slightly if you like.

5. *For a ribbon edge:* trim the dough even with the rim and press it flat. Cut long strips about 2cm/¾in wide from the dough trimmings. Moisten the edge and press one end of a strip on to it. Twist the strip gently and press it on to the edge again. Continue all the way round the edge.

Gelatine

DISSOLVING GELATINE

It's important to dissolve gelatine correctly, or it can spoil the texture and set of your finished dessert.

1 Place 45ml/3 tbsp of very hot water per sachet of gelatine in a small bowl.

2 Sprinkle the gelatine over the liquid. Always add the gelatine to the liquid, never the other way round.

3 Stir briskly until the gelatine is completely dissolved. There should be no visible crystals and the liquid should be clear. If necessary, stand the container in a pan of hot water over a low heat until dissolved. Do not allow the gelatine to boil.

VEGETARIAN ALTERNATIVE

There is a vegetarian alternative to gelatine, which can be used in the appropriate recipes, if you wish. Follow the instructions on the packet, but in general you should sprinkle the alternative on to cold liquids and stir until completely dissolved. Next, heat the mixture to near boiling. (If setting proves difficult add more of the gelatine alternative to the mixture and reheat.) It is now ready to be used as specified in the recipe, but should be allowed to set for about 1 hour, or until firm, and should always be allowed to cool.

Redcurrant and Raspberry Coulis

A dessert sauce for the height of summer to serve with light meringues and fruit sorbets. Make it particularly pretty with a decoration of fresh flowers and leaves.

INGREDIENTS

Serves 6

225g/8oz/2 cups redcurrants
450g/1lb/2⅔ cups raspberries
50g/2oz/½ cup icing (confectioners') sugar
15ml/1 tbsp cornflour (cornstarch)
juice of 1 orange
30ml/2 tbsp double (heavy) cream, to decorate

1 Strip the redcurrants from their stalks using a fork. Place in a food processor or blender with the raspberries and sugar, and purée until it is smooth.

2 Press the mixture through a fine sieve into a bowl and discard the seeds and pulp.

3 Blend the cornflour with the orange juice then stir into the fruit purée. Transfer to a pan and bring to the boil, stirring continuously, and cook for 1–2 minutes until smooth and thick. Set aside until cold.

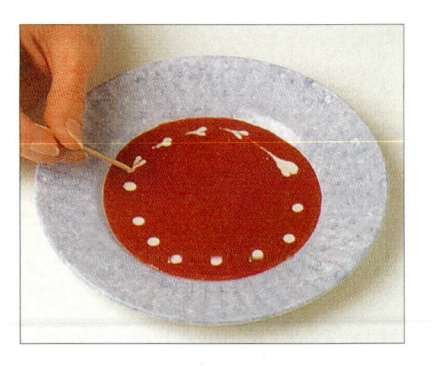

4 Spoon the sauce over each plate. Drip the cream from a teaspoon to make small dots evenly around the edge. Draw a cocktail stick (toothpick) through the dots to form heart shapes. Place the meringue or scoop sorbet into the middle and decorate with flowers.

Crème Anglaise

Here is the classic English custard, light, creamy and delicious – far superior to packet versions. Serve hot or cold.

INGREDIENTS

Serves 4

1 vanilla pod (bean)
450ml/¾ pint/1⅞ cups milk
40g/1½oz/3 tbsp caster (superfine) sugar
4 egg yolks

1 Split the vanilla pod and place in a pan with the milk. Bring slowly to the boil. Remove from the heat, then cover and infuse for 10 minutes before removing the pod.

2 Beat together the sugar and egg yolks until thick, light and creamy.

3 Slowly pour the warm milk on to the egg mixture, stirring constantly.

4 Transfer to the top of a double boiler or place the bowl over a pan of hot water. Stir constantly over a low heat for 10 minutes, or until the mixture coats the back of the spoon. Remove from the heat immediately as curdling will occur if the custard is allowed to simmer.

5 Strain the custard into a jug if serving hot or, if serving cold, strain into a bowl and cover the surface with buttered paper or clear film (plastic wrap).

VARIATION

Infuse a few strips of thinly pared lemon or orange rind with the milk, instead of the vanilla pod.

Sabayon

Serve this frothy sauce hot over steamed puddings or chill and serve just as it is with light dessert cookies, or whatever you prefer. Never let it stand for any length of time, as it will collapse.

INGREDIENTS

Serves 4–6

1 egg
2 egg yolks
75g/3oz/⅔ cup caster (superfine) sugar
150ml/¼ pint/⅔ cups sweet white wine
finely grated rind and juice of 1 lemon

1 Whisk the egg, yolks and sugar until they are pale and thick.

2 Stand the bowl over a pan of hot – not boiling – water. Add the wine and lemon juice, a little at a time, whisking vigorously.

3 Continue whisking until the mixture is thick enough to leave a trail. Whisk in the lemon rind. If serving hot, serve immediately over pudding or fruit salad.

4 To serve cold, place over a bowl of iced water and whisk until chilled. Pour into small glasses and serve immediately.

Butterscotch Sauce

A deliciously sweet sauce which will be loved by adults and children alike! Serve with ice cream or with pancakes or waffles.

INGREDIENTS

Serves 4–6

75g/3oz/6 tbsp unsalted butter
175g/6oz/¾ cup soft dark brown sugar
175ml/6fl oz/¾ cup evaporated milk
50g/2oz/½ cup hazelnuts

1 Melt the butter and sugar in a heavy pan, bring to the boil and boil for 2 minutes. Cool for 5 minutes.

2 Heat the evaporated milk to just below boiling point, then gradually stir into the sugar mixture. Cook over a low heat for 2 minutes, stirring frequently.

3 Spread the hazelnuts on a baking sheet and toast in a hot oven.

4 Tip the nuts on to a clean dish towel and rub them briskly to remove the skins.

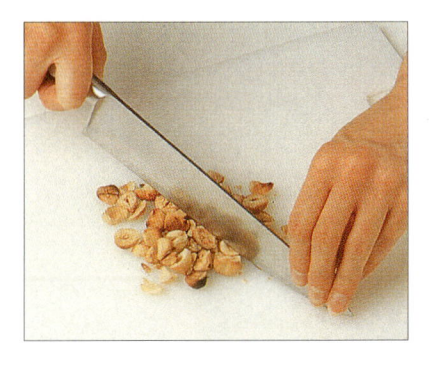

5 Chop the nuts roughly and stir into the sauce. Serve hot, poured over scoops of vanilla ice cream and warm waffles or pancakes.

Brandy Butter

This is traditionally served with Christmas pudding and mince pies but a good spoonful on a hot baked apple is equally delicious.

INGREDIENTS

Serves 6

100g/4oz/½ cup butter
100g/4oz/½ cup icing (confectioners'), caster (superfine), or light brown sugar
45ml/3 tbsp brandy

1 Cream the butter until very pale and soft. Beat in the sugar gradually.

2 Add the brandy, a few drops at a time, beating continuously. Add enough for a good flavour but take care it does not curdle.

3 Pile into a small serving dish and allow to harden. Alternatively, spread on to foil and chill until firm. Cut into shapes with small fancy cutters.

VARIATION

Cumberland Rum Butter
Use soft light brown sugar and rum instead of brandy. Beat in the grated rind of 1 orange and a good pinch of mixed (pumpkin pie) spice with the sugar.

Chocolate Fudge Sauce

A real treat if you're not counting calories. Fabulous with scoops of vanilla ice cream.

INGREDIENTS

Serves 6

150ml/¼ pint/⅔ cup double (heavy) cream
50g/2oz/4 tbsp butter
50g/2oz/¼ cup granulated sugar
175g/6oz plain (semisweet) chocolate
30ml/2 tbsp brandy

VARIATIONS

White Chocolate and Orange Sauce:
40g/1½oz/3 tbsp caster (superfine) sugar, to replace granulated sugar
175g/6oz white chocolate, to replace plain chocolate
30ml/2 tbsp orange liqueur, to replace brandy
finely grated rind of 1 orange

Coffee Chocolate Fudge:
50g/2oz/¼ cup soft light brown sugar, to replace granulated sugar
30ml/2 tbsp coffee liqueur or dark rum, to replace brandy
15ml/1 tbsp coffee essence

1 Heat the cream with the butter and sugar in the top of a double boiler or in a heatproof bowl over a pan of hot water. Stir until smooth, then cool.

2 Break the chocolate into the cream. Stir until it is melted and thoroughly combined.

3 Stir in the brandy a little at a time, then cool to room temperature.

4 For the White Chocolate and Orange Sauce, heat the cream and butter with the sugar and orange rind in the top of a double boiler, until dissolved. Then, follow the recipe to the end, but using white chocolate and orange liqueur instead.

5 For the Coffee Chocolate Fudge, follow the recipe, using light brown sugar and coffee liqueur or rum. Stir in the coffee essence at the end.

6 Serve the sauce over cream-filled profiteroles, and serve any that is left over separately.

Glossy Chocolate Sauce

Delicious poured over ice cream or on hot or cold desserts, this sauce also freezes well. Pour into a freezer-proof container, seal, and keep for up to three months. Thaw at room temperature.

INGREDIENTS

Serves 6

115g/4oz/½ cup caster (superfine) sugar
175g/6oz plain (semisweet) chocolate, broken into squares
30ml/2 tbsp unsalted butter
30ml/2 tbsp brandy or orange juice

1 Place the sugar and 60ml/4 tbsp of water in a pan and heat gently, stirring occasionally, until the sugar has dissolved.

2 Stir in the chocolate, a few squares at a time, until melted, then add the butter in the same way. Do not allow the sauce to boil. Stir in the brandy or orange juice and serve warm.

Cold Desserts

Double Chocolate Snowball

This is an ideal party dessert as it can be prepared the day before and decorated on the day.

INGREDIENTS

Serves 12–14

350g/12oz plain (semisweet) chocolate, chopped

285g/10½oz/1½ cups caster (superfine) sugar

275g/10oz/1¼ cups unsalted butter, cut into small pieces

8 eggs

50ml/2fl oz/¼ cup orange-flavoured liqueur or brandy (optional)

cocoa, for dusting (optional)

For the white chocolate cream

200g/7oz white chocolate, chopped

475ml/16fl oz/2 cups double (heavy) or whipping cream

30ml/2 tbsp orange-flavoured liqueur (optional)

1 Preheat the oven to 180°C/350°F/Gas 4. Line a 1.75 litre/3 pint round ovenproof bowl with aluminium foil, smoothing the sides. In a bowl over a pan of simmering water, melt the plain chocolate. Add the sugar and stir until it dissolves. Strain into a medium bowl. With an electric mixer at low speed, beat in the butter, then the eggs, one at a time, beating well after each addition. Stir in the liqueur or brandy, if using, and pour into the prepared bowl. Tap gently to release any large air bubbles.

2 Bake for 1¼–1½ hours until the surface is firm and slightly risen, but cracked. The centre will still be wobbly: this will set on cooling. Remove to a rack to cool to room temperature. Cover with a plate, then cover completely with clear film (plastic wrap) or foil and chill overnight. To unmould, remove plate and film or foil and invert mould on to a plate; shake firmly to release. Peel off foil. Cover until ready to decorate.

3 Process the white chocolate in a blender or food processor until fine crumbs form. In a small pan, heat 120ml/4fl oz/½ cup of the cream until just beginning to simmer. With the food processor running, pour the cream through the feed tube and process until the chocolate is completely melted. Strain into a medium bowl and cool to room temperature, stirring occasionally.

4 Beat the remaining cream until soft peaks form, add the liqueur, if using, and beat for 30 seconds or until the cream just holds its shape. Fold a spoonful of cream into the chocolate then fold in remaining cream. Spoon into a piping (icing) bag fitted with a star tip and pipe rosettes over the surface. If desired, dust with cocoa.

Chocolate Mandarin Trifle

Trifle is always a tempting treat, but when a rich chocolate and mascarpone custard is combined with amaretto and mandarin oranges, it becomes irresistible.

INGREDIENTS

Serves 6–8

4 trifle sponges
14 amaretti biscuits or almond cookies
60ml/4 tbsp Amaretto di Saronno or sweet sherry
8 mandarin oranges

For the custard
200g/7oz plain (semisweet) chocolate, broken into squares
30ml/2 tbsp cornflour (cornstarch) or custard powder
30ml/2 tbsp caster (superfine) sugar
2 egg yolks
200ml/7fl oz/⅞ cup milk
250g/9oz/generous 1 cup mascarpone

For the topping
250g/9oz/generous 1 cup fromage frais or mascarpone
chocolate shapes
mandarin slices

1 Break up the trifle sponges and place them in a large glass serving dish. Crumble the amaretti biscuits over and then sprinkle with amaretto or sweet sherry.

2 Squeeze the juice from 2 of the mandarins and sprinkle into the dish. Segment the rest and put in the dish.

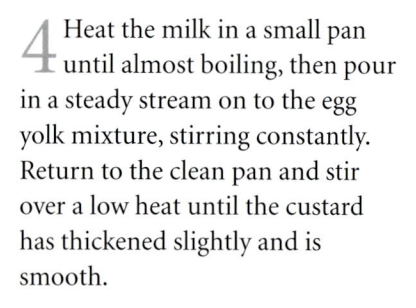

3 Make the custard. Melt the chocolate in a heatproof bowl over hot water. In a separate bowl, mix the cornflour or custard powder, sugar and egg yolks to a smooth paste.

4 Heat the milk in a small pan until almost boiling, then pour in a steady stream on to the egg yolk mixture, stirring constantly. Return to the clean pan and stir over a low heat until the custard has thickened slightly and is smooth.

5 Stir in the mascarpone until melted, then add the melted chocolate, mixing it thoroughly. Spread evenly over the trifle, cool, then chill until set.

6 To finish, spread the fromage frais over the custard, then decorate with chocolate shapes and the remaining mandarin slices just before serving.

COOK'S TIP

Always use the best chocolate which has a high percentage of cocoa solids, and take care not to overheat the chocolate when melting as it will lose its gloss and look "grainy".

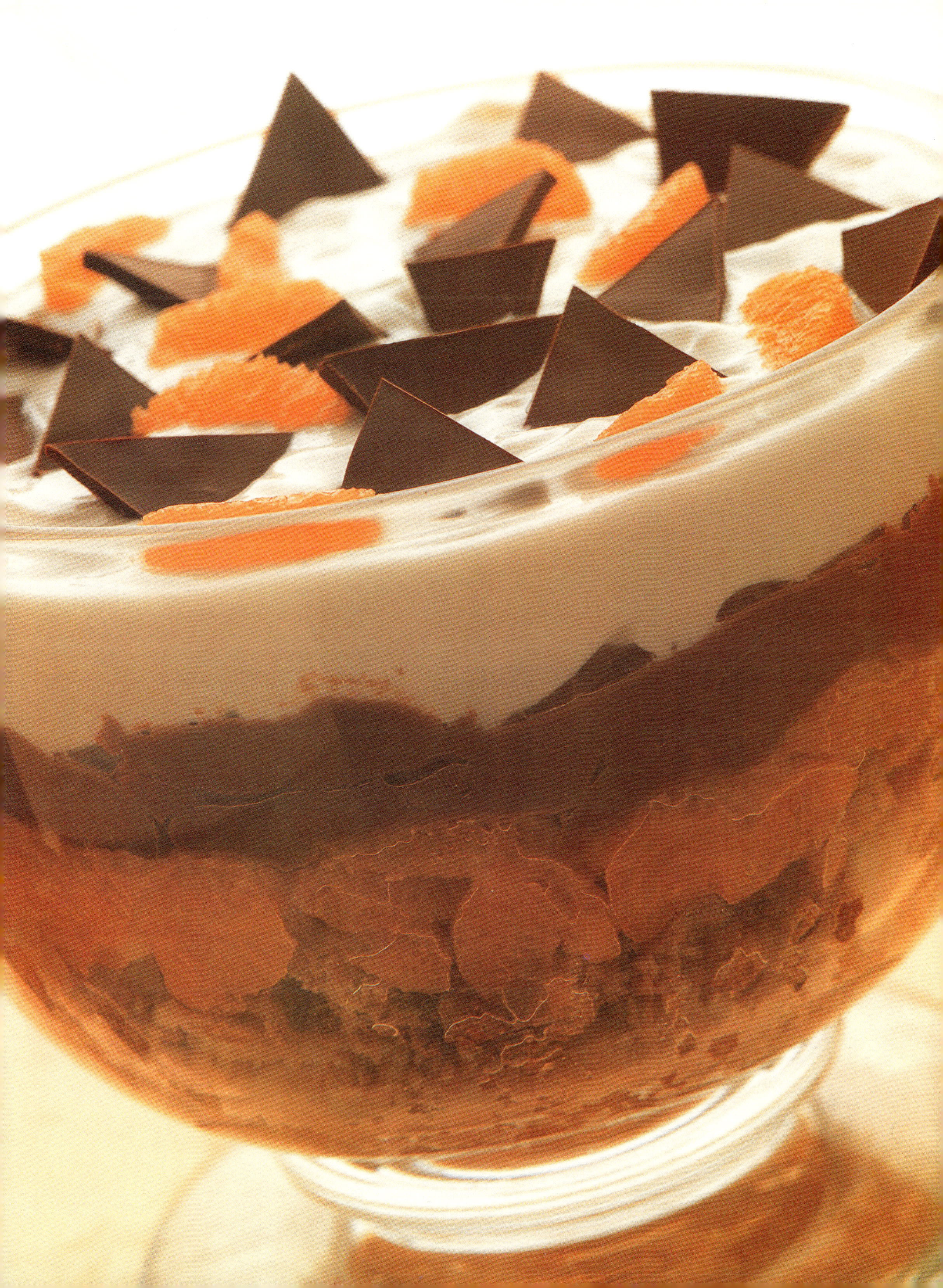

White Chocolate Parfait

Everything you could wish for in a dessert; white and dark chocolate in one mouth-watering slice.

INGREDIENTS

Serves 10

225g/8oz white chocolate, chopped
600ml/1 pint/2½ cups whipping cream
120ml/4fl oz/½ cup milk
10 egg yolks
15ml/1 tbsp caster (superfine) sugar
25g/1oz/scant ½ cup desiccated (dry unsweetened shredded) coconut
120ml/4fl oz/½ cup canned sweetened coconut milk
150g/5oz/1¼ cups unsalted macadamia nuts

For the chocolate icing
225g/8oz plain (semisweet) chocolate
75g/3oz/6 tbsp butter
20ml/1 tbsp golden (light corn) syrup
175ml/6fl oz/¾ cup whipping cream
curls of fresh coconut, to decorate

1 Line the base and sides of a 1.4 litre/2⅓ pint/6 cup terrine mould (25 x 10cm/10 x 4in) with clear film (plastic wrap).

2 Place the chopped white chocolate and 50ml/2fl oz/ ½ cup of the cream in the top of a double boiler or in a heatproof bowl set over hot water. Stir until melted and smooth. Set aside.

3 Put 250ml/8fl oz/1 cup of the cream and the milk in a pan and bring to boiling point.

4 Meanwhile, whisk the egg yolks and caster sugar together in a large bowl, until thick and pale.

5 Add the hot cream mixture to the yolks, beating constantly. Pour back into the pan and cook over a low heat for 2–3 minutes, until thickened. Stir constantly and do not boil. Remove the pan from the heat.

6 Add the melted chocolate, desiccated coconut and coconut milk, then stir well and leave to cool.

7 Whip the remaining cream until thick, then fold into the chocolate and coconut mixture.

8 Put 475ml/16fl oz/2 cups of the parfait mixture in the prepared mould and spread evenly. Cover and freeze for about 2 hours, until just firm. Cover the remaining mixture and chill.

9 Sprinkle the macadamia nuts evenly over the frozen parfait. Pour in the remaining parfait mixture. Cover the terrine and freeze for 6–8 hours or overnight, until the parfait is firm.

10 To make the icing, melt the chocolate with the butter and syrup in the top of a double boiler set over hot water. Stir occasionally.

11 Heat the cream in a pan, until just simmering, then stir into the chocolate mixture. Remove the pan from the heat and leave to cool until lukewarm.

12 To turn out the parfait, wrap the terrine in a hot towel and set it upside-down on a plate. Lift off the terrine mould, then peel off the clear film (plastic wrap). Place the parfait on a rack over a baking sheet and pour the chocolate icing evenly over the top. Working quickly, smooth the icing down the sides with a spatula. Leave to set slightly, then freeze for a further 3–4 hours. Cut into slices using a knife dipped in hot water. Serve, decorated with curls of fresh coconut.

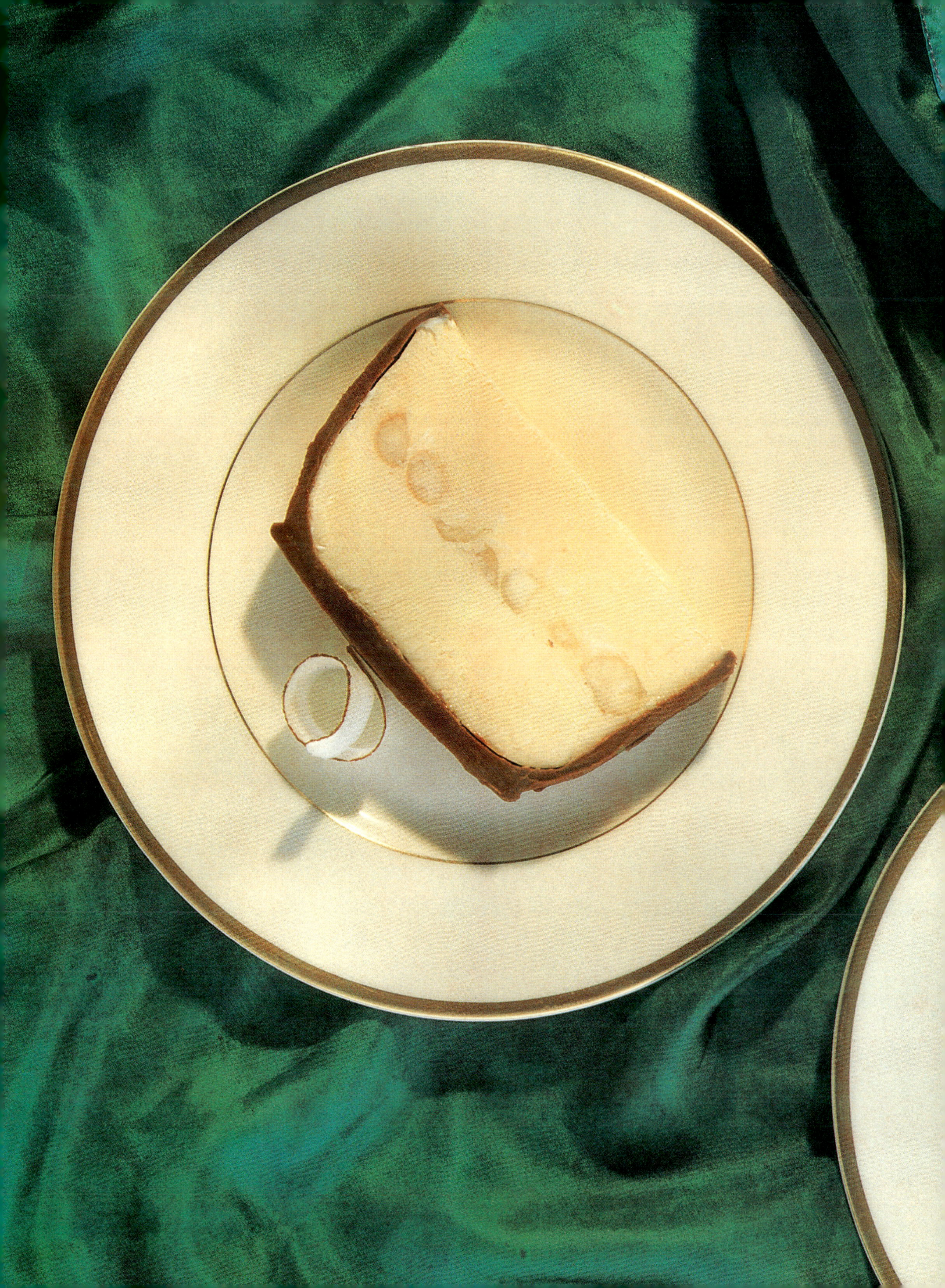

White Chocolate Mousse with Dark Sauce

Creamy vanilla-flavoured white chocolate mousse is served with a dark rum and chocolate sauce.

INGREDIENTS

Serves 6–8

200g/7oz white chocolate, broken into squares
2 eggs, separated
60ml/4 tbsp caster (superfine) sugar
300ml/½ pint/1¼ cups double (heavy) cream
1 sachet powdered gelatine or alternative
150ml/¼ pint/⅔ cup plain yogurt
10ml/2 tsp vanilla essence (extract)

For the sauce

50g/2oz plain (semisweet) chocolate, broken into squares
30ml/2 tbsp dark rum
60ml/4 tbsp single (light) cream

1 Line a 1 litre/1¾ pint/4 cup loaf tin (pan) with baking parchment or clear film (plastic wrap). Melt the chocolate in a heatproof bowl over hot water, then remove from the heat.

2 Whisk the egg yolks and sugar in a bowl until pale and thick, then beat in the melted chocolate.

3 Heat the cream in a small pan until almost boiling, then remove from the heat. Sprinkle the gelatine over, stirring gently until it is completely dissolved.

4 Then pour on to the chocolate mixture, whisking vigorously to mix until smooth.

5 Whisk the yogurt and vanilla essence into the mixture. In a clean, grease-free bowl, whisk the egg whites until stiff, then fold them into the mixture. Tip into the prepared loaf tin, level the surface and chill until set.

6 Make the sauce. Melt the chocolate with the rum and cream in a heatproof bowl over barely simmering water, stirring occasionally, then leave to cool.

7 When the mousse is set, remove it from the tin with the aid of the paper or clear film. Serve in thick slices with the cooled chocolate sauce poured around.

COOK'S TIP

Make sure the gelatine is completely dissolved in the cream before adding to the other ingredients.

Raspberry and White Chocolate Cheesecake

An irresistible combination of raspberries and white chocolate on a crunchy ginger and pecan nut base.

INGREDIENTS

Serves 8

50g/2oz/4 tbsp unsalted butter

225g/8oz/2⅓ cups ginger nut biscuits, crushed

50g/2oz/½ cup chopped pecan nuts or walnuts

For the filling

275g/10oz/1¼ cups mascarpone cheese

175g/6oz/¾ cup fromage frais or cream cheese

2 eggs, beaten

45ml/3 tbsp caster (superfine) sugar

250g/9oz white chocolate, broken into squares

225g/8oz/1⅓ cups fresh or frozen raspberries

For the topping

115g/4oz/½ cup mascarpone cheese

75g/3oz/⅓ cup fromage frais or whipped cream

white chocolate curls and raspberries, to decorate

1 Preheat the oven to 150°C/300°F/Gas 2. Melt the butter in a pan, then stir in the crushed biscuits and nuts. Press into the base of a 23cm/9in springform cake tin (pan).

2 Make the filling. Beat the mascarpone and fromage frais or cream cheese in a bowl, then beat in the eggs and caster sugar.

3 Melt the white chocolate gently in a heatproof bowl over hot water.

4 Stir the chocolate into the cheese mixture with the raspberries.

5 Tip into the prepared tin and spread evenly, then bake for about 1 hour or until just set. Switch off the oven, but do not remove the cheesecake. Leave it until cold and completely set.

6 Release the tin and lift the cheesecake on to a plate. Make the topping by mixing the mascarpone and fromage frais, or cream, in a bowl and spread over the cheesecake. Decorate with chocolate curls and raspberries.

Classic Cheesecake

Serve this with cream, if you like, but it tastes delicious just as it is.

INGREDIENTS

Serves 8

25g/1oz/½ cup digestive biscuit (Graham cracker) crumbs
900g/2lb cream cheese
250g/9oz/1¼ cups caster (superfine) sugar
grated rind of 1 lemon
45ml/3 tbsp fresh lemon juice
5ml/1 tsp vanilla essence (extract)
4 eggs, at room temperature

1 Preheat the oven to 160°C/325°F/Gas 3. Grease a 23cm/8in springform cake tin (pan). Place on a round of foil 13cm/5in larger than the diameter of the tin. Press it up the sides to seal tightly.

2 Sprinkle the crumbs in the base of the tin. Press to form an even layer.

3 With an electric mixer, beat the cream cheese until smooth. Add the sugar, lemon rind and juice and vanilla essence, and beat until blended. Beat in the eggs, one at a time. Beat just enough to blend thoroughly.

4 Pour into the prepared tin. Set the tin in a larger baking tray and place in the oven. Pour enough hot water in the outer tray to come 2.5cm/1in up the side of the tin.

5 Bake until the top of the cake is golden brown, about 1½ hours. Let cool in the tin.

6 Run a knife around the edge to loosen, then remove the rim of the tin. Chill for at least 4 hours before serving.

Chocolate Cheesecake

This popular variation of the classic dessert is flavoured with cinnamon.

INGREDIENTS

Serves 10–12

175g/6oz plain (semisweet) chocolate
115g/4oz bitter chocolate
1.15kg/2½lb cream cheese, at room temperature
200g/7oz/1 cup caster (superfine) sugar
10ml/2 tsp vanilla essence (extract)
4 eggs, at room temperature
175ml/6fl oz/¾ cup sour cream

For the base
75g/3oz/1½ cups chocolate wafer crumbs
75g/3oz/6 tbsp butter, melted
2.5ml/½ tsp ground cinnamon

1 Preheat the oven to 180°C/350°F/Gas 4. Grease a 23cm/9in springform cake tin (pan).

2 For the base, mix the chocolate wafer crumbs with the butter and cinnamon. Press evenly in the bottom of the tin.

3 Break up and melt the plain and bitter chocolate in the top of a double boiler, or in a heatproof bowl set over hot water. Set aside.

4 With an electric mixer, beat the cream cheese until smooth, then beat in the sugar and vanilla essence. Add the eggs, one at a time, scraping the bowl with a spatula when necessary.

5 Add the sour cream. Stir in the melted chocolate.

6 Pour into the tin and bake for 1 hour. Allow to cool in the tin. Remove the rim and chill before serving.

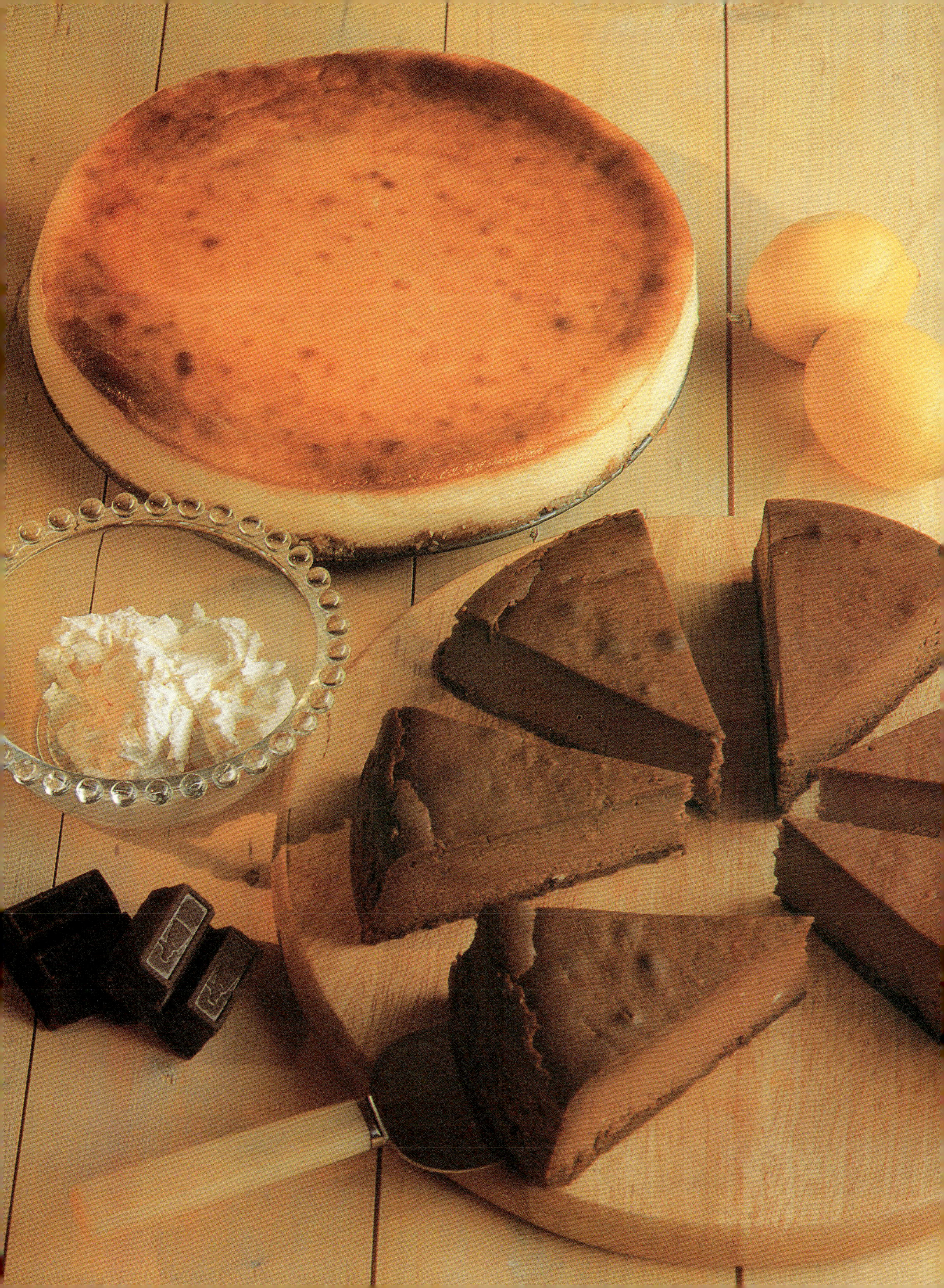

Chocolate Profiteroles

This mouth-watering dessert is served in cafés throughout France. Sometimes the profiteroles are filled with whipped cream instead of ice cream, but they are always drizzled with chocolate sauce.

INGREDIENTS

Serves 4–6

275g/10oz plain (semisweet) chocolate
750ml/1¼ pints/3 cups vanilla ice cream

For the profiteroles
110g/3¾oz/¾ cup plain (all-purpose) flour
1.5ml/¼ tsp salt
pinch of freshly grated nutmeg
75g/3oz/6 tbsp unsalted butter, cut into pieces
3 eggs

1 Preheat the oven to 200°C/400°F/Gas 6 and butter a baking sheet.

2 To make the profiteroles, sift together the flour, salt and nutmeg. In a medium pan, bring the butter and 175ml/6fl oz/¾ cup of water to the boil. Remove from the heat and add the dry ingredients all at once. Beat with a wooden spoon for about 1 minute until well blended and the mixture starts to pull away from the sides of the pan, then set the pan over a low heat and cook the mixture for about 2 minutes, beating constantly. Remove from the heat.

3 Beat one egg in a small bowl and set aside. Add the remaining eggs, one at a time, to the flour mixture, beating well. Add the beaten egg gradually until the dough is smooth and shiny; it should fall slowly when dropped from a spoon.

4 Using a tablespoon, drop the dough on to the baking sheet in 12 mounds. Bake for 25–30 minutes until the pastry is well risen and browned. Turn off the oven and leave the puffs to cool with the oven door open.

5 To make the sauce, place the chocolate and 120ml/4fl oz/½ cup of warm water in a double boiler or in a bowl over a pan of hot water and melt, stirring occasionally.

6 Split the profiteroles in half and put a small scoop of ice cream in each. Arrange on a serving platter. Pour the sauce over and serve immediately.

Australian Hazelnut Pavlova

Meringue topped with fresh fruit and cream – perfect for summer dinner parties.

INGREDIENTS

Serves 4–6

3 egg whites
175g/6oz/generous ¾ cup caster (superfine) sugar
5ml/1 tsp cornflour (cornstarch)
5ml/1 tsp white wine vinegar
40g/1½oz/5 tbsp chopped roasted hazelnuts
250ml/8fl oz/1 cup double (heavy) cream
15ml/1 tbsp orange juice
30ml/2 tbsp natural thick and creamy yogurt
2 ripe nectarines, stoned (pitted) and sliced
225g/8oz/1⅓ cups raspberries
15–30ml/1–2 tbsp redcurrant jelly, warmed

1 Preheat the oven to 140°C/275°F/Gas 1. Lightly grease a baking sheet. Draw a 20cm/8in circle on a sheet of baking parchment. Place pencil-side down on the baking sheet.

2 Place the egg whites in a clean, grease-free bowl and whisk with an electric mixer until stiff. Whisk in the sugar 15ml/1 tbsp at a time, whisking well after each addition.

3 Add the cornflour, vinegar and hazelnuts and fold in carefully with a large metal spoon.

4 Spoon the meringue on to the marked circle and spread out, making a depression in the centre.

5 Bake for about 1¼–1½ hours, until crisp. Leave to cool, then transfer to a serving platter.

6 Whip the cream and orange juice until just thick, stir in the yogurt and spoon on to the meringue. Top with the fruit and drizzle over the redcurrant jelly. Serve immediately.

Blackcurrant Sorbet

Blackcurrants make a vibrant and intensely flavoured sorbet.

INGREDIENTS

Serves 4–6

90g/3½oz/½ cup caster (superfine) sugar
500g/1¼lb/5 cups blackcurrants
juice of ½ lemon
15ml/1 tbsp egg white
mint sprigs, to decorate

1 In a small pan over a medium-high heat, bring the sugar and 120ml/4fl oz/½ cup of water to the boil, stirring until the sugar dissolves. Boil the syrup for 2 minutes, then remove the pan from the heat and set aside to cool.

2 Remove the blackcurrants from the stalks, by pulling them through the tines of a fork.

3 In a blender or food processor fitted with a metal blade, process the blackcurrants and lemon juice until smooth. Alternatively, chop the blackcurrants coarsely, then add the lemon juice. Mix in the sugar syrup.

4 Press the purée through a sieve to remove the seeds.

5 Pour the blackcurrant purée into a non-metallic, freezer-proof dish. Cover the dish with clear film (plastic wrap) or a lid and freeze until the sorbet is nearly firm, but still a bit slushy.

6 Cut the sorbet into pieces and put into the blender or food processor. Process until smooth, then with the machine running, add the egg white and process until well mixed. Tip the sorbet back into the dish and freeze until almost firm. Chop the sorbet again and process until smooth.

7 Serve immediately or freeze, tightly covered, for up to 1 week. Allow to soften for 5–10 minutes at room temperature before serving, decorated with mint sprigs.

Lemon Soufflé with Blackberry Sauce

The simple fresh taste of cold lemon soufflé combines well with the rich blackberry sauce, and the colour contrast looks good, too. Blueberries or raspberries make delicious alternatives to blackberries.

INGREDIENTS

Serves 6

grated rind of 1 lemon and juice of 2 lemons
15ml/1 tbsp/1 sachet powdered gelatine
5 small (US medium) eggs, separated
150g/5oz/¾ cup caster (superfine) sugar
few drops vanilla essence (extract)
400ml/14fl oz/1⅔ cups whipping cream

For the sauce
175g/6oz/¾ cup blackberries (fresh or frozen)
30–45ml/2–3 tbsp caster sugar
few fresh blackberries and blackberry leaves, to decorate

1 Place the lemon juice in a small pan and heat through. Sprinkle on the gelatine and leave to dissolve or heat further until clear. Allow to cool.

2 Put the lemon rind, egg yolks, sugar and vanilla into a large bowl and whisk until the mixture is very thick, pale and creamy.

3 Whisk the egg whites until stiff and almost peaky. Whip the cream until stiff.

4 Stir the gelatine mixture into the yolks, then fold in the whipped cream and lastly the egg whites. Turn into a 1.5 litre/2½ pint/6 cup soufflé dish and freeze for about 2 hours.

5 To make the sauce, place the blackberries in a pan with the sugar and cook for 4–6 minutes, until the juices begin to run and all the sugar has dissolved. Pass through a sieve to remove the seeds, then chill.

6 When the soufflé is almost frozen, but still spoonable, scoop or spoon out on to individual plates and serve with the blackberry sauce, decorated with fresh blackberries and blackberry leaves.

Apricots with Orange Cream

Mascarpone is a very rich cream cheese made from thick Lombardy cream. It is delicious flavoured with orange as a topping for these poached, chilled apricots.

INGREDIENTS

Serves 4

450g/1lb/2 cups ready-to-eat dried apricots
strip of orange peel
1 cinnamon stick
45ml/3 tbsp caster (superfine) sugar
150ml/¼ pint/⅔ cup sweet dessert wine
115g/4oz/½ cup mascarpone
45ml/3 tbsp orange juice
pinch of ground cinnamon and fresh mint sprig, to decorate

1 Place the apricots, orange peel, cinnamon stick and 15ml/1 tbsp of the sugar in a pan and cover with 450ml/¼ pint/1⅞ cups cold water. Bring to the boil, cover and simmer gently for 25 minutes, until the fruit is tender.

2 Remove from the heat and stir in the dessert wine. Leave until cold, then chill for at least 3–4 hours or overnight.

3 Mix together the mascarpone, orange juice and the remaining sugar in a bowl and beat well until smooth, then chill.

4 Just before serving remove the cinnamon stick and orange peel and serve with a spoonful of the orange cream sprinkled with cinnamon and decorated with a sprig of fresh mint.

Rhubarb and Orange Fool

Perhaps this traditional English pudding got its name because it is so easy to make that even a "fool" can attempt it.

INGREDIENTS

Serves 4

30ml/2 tbsp orange juice
5ml/1 tsp finely shredded orange rind
1kg/2lb (about 10–12 stems) rhubarb, chopped
15ml/1 tbsp redcurrant jelly
45ml/3 tbsp caster (superfine) sugar
150g/5oz/⅔ cup ready-to-serve thick and creamy custard
150ml/¼ pint/⅔ cup double (heavy) cream, whipped
sweet biscuits (cookies), to serve

1 Place the orange juice and rind, the chopped rhubarb, redcurrant jelly and sugar in a pan. Cover and simmer gently for about 8 minutes, stirring occasionally, until the rhubarb is just tender but not mushy.

2 Remove the pan from the heat, transfer the rhubarb to a bowl and leave to cool completely.

3 Drain the cooled rhubarb to remove some of the liquid. Reserve a few pieces of the rhubarb and a little orange rind for decoration. Purée the remaining rhubarb in a food processor or blender, or press through a sieve.

4 Stir the custard into the purée, then fold in the whipped cream. Spoon the fool into individual bowls, cover and chill. Just before serving, top with the reserved fruit and rind. Serve with crisp, sweet biscuits.

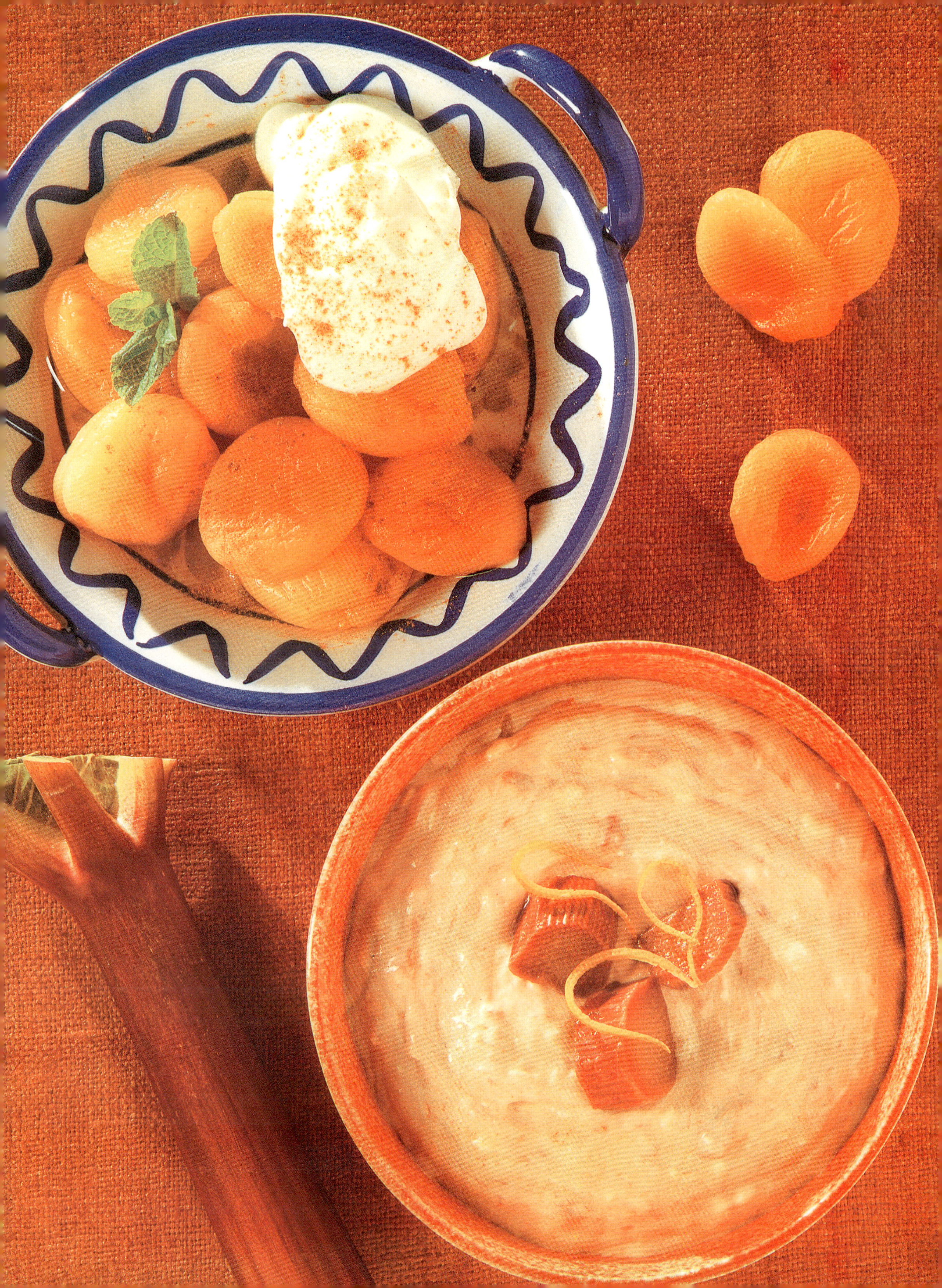

Iced Praline Torte

Make this elaborate torte several days ahead, decorate it and return it to the freezer until you are nearly ready to serve it. Allow the torte to stand at room temperature for an hour before serving, or leave it in the refrigerator overnight to soften.

INGREDIENTS

Serves 8

115g/4oz/1 cup almonds or hazelnuts
115g/4oz/8 tbsp caster (superfine) sugar
115g/4oz/⅔ cup raisins
90ml/6 tbsp rum or brandy
115g/4oz dark chocolate,
30ml/2 tbsp milk
450ml/¾ pint/1⅞ cups double (heavy) cream
30ml/2 tbsp strong black coffee
16 sponge-finger biscuits (ladyfingers)

To finish
150ml/¼ pint/⅔ cup double cream
50g/2oz/½ cup flaked (sliced) almonds, toasted
15g/½oz dark chocolate, melted

1 To make the praline, have ready an oiled baking sheet. Put the almonds or hazelnuts into a heavy pan with the sugar and heat gently until the sugar melts. Swirl the pan to coat the nuts in the hot sugar. Cook slowly until the nuts brown and the sugar caramelizes. Transfer the nuts quickly to baking sheet and leave them to cool completely. Break them up and grind them to a fine powder in a blender or food processor.

2 Soak the raisins in 45ml/3 tbsp of the rum or brandy for an hour (or better still overnight), so they soften. Melt the chocolate with the milk in a bowl over a pan of hot, but not boiling water. Remove and allow to cool. Lightly grease a 1.2 litre/ 2 pint/5 cup loaf tin (pan) and line it with greaseproof (waxed) paper.

3 Whisk the cream in a bowl until it holds soft peaks. Whisk in the cold chocolate. Then fold in the praline and the soaked raisins, with any liquid.

4 Mix the coffee and remaining rum or brandy in a shallow dish. Dip in the sponge-fingers and arrange half in a layer over the base of the prepared loaf tin.

5 Cover with the chocolate mixture and add another layer of soaked sponge-fingers. Leave in the freezer overnight.

6 Whip the double cream for the topping. Dip the tin briefly into warm water to loosen it and turn the torte out on to a serving plate. Cover with the whipped cream, sprinkle the top with toasted flaked almonds and drizzle the melted chocolate over the top. Return the torte to the freezer until it is needed.

COOK'S TIP

Make the praline in advance and store it in an airtight jar until needed.

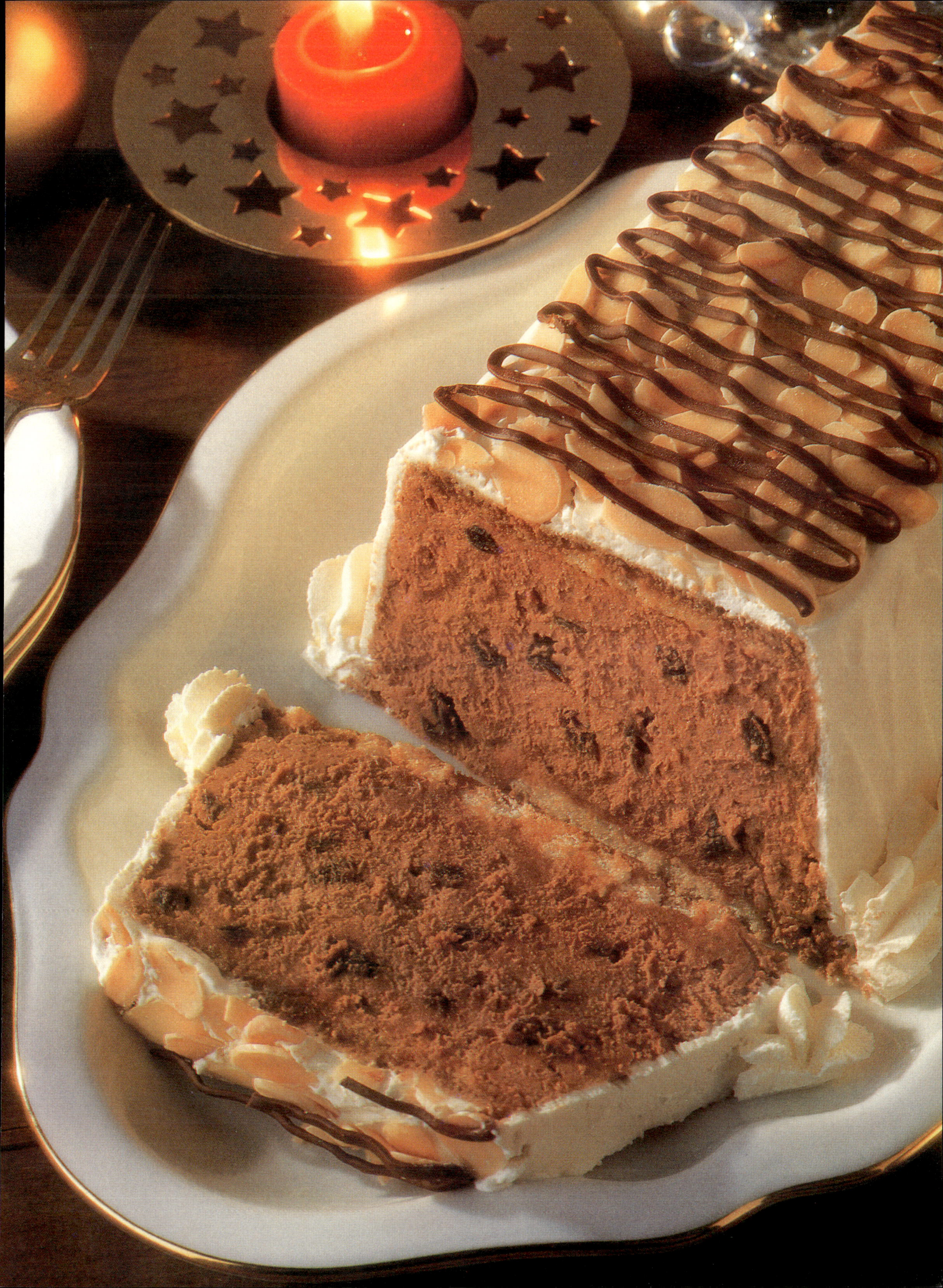

Indian Ice Cream (Kulfi)

Kulfi-wallahs (ice cream vendors) have always made kulfi, and continue to this day, without using modern freezers, but this method works well in an ordinary freezer.

INGREDIENTS

Serves 4–6

3 x 400ml/14fl oz cans evaporated milk
3 egg whites, whisked until peaks form
350g/12oz/3 cups icing (confectioners') sugar
5ml/1 tsp cardamom powder
15ml/1 tbsp rose water
175g/6oz/1½ cups pistachios, chopped
75g/3oz/generous ½ cup sultanas (golden raisins)
75g/3oz/¾ cup flaked (sliced) almonds
25g/1oz/2 tbsp glacé (candied) cherries, halved

1 Remove the labels from the cans of evaporated milk and lay the cans down in a pan with a tight-fitting cover. Fill the pan with water to reach three-quarters up the cans. Bring to the boil, cover and simmer for 20 minutes. When cool, remove and chill the cans in the fridge for 24 hours.

2 Open the cans and empty the milk into a large, chilled bowl. Whisk until it doubles in quantity, then fold in the whisked egg whites and icing sugar.

3 Gently fold in the remaining ingredients, seal the bowl with clear film (plastic wrap) and leave in the freezer for 1 hour.

4 Remove the ice cream from the freezer and mix well with a fork. Transfer to a freezer container and return to the freezer for a final setting. Remove from the freezer 10 minutes before serving in scoops.

Mocha Cream Pots

The name of this rich baked custard, a classic French dessert, comes from the baking cups, called pots de crème.

INGREDIENTS

Serves 8

15ml/1 tbsp instant coffee powder
475ml/16fl oz/2 cups milk
75g/3oz/⅓ cup caster (superfine) sugar
225g/8oz plain (semisweet) chocolate,
10ml/2 tsp vanilla essence (extract)
30ml/2 tbsp coffee liqueur (optional)
7 egg yolks
whipped cream and crystallized mimosa balls, to decorate (optional)

1 Preheat the oven to 160°C/325°F/Gas 3. Place eight 120ml/4fl oz/½ cup *pots de crème* cups or ramekins in a roasting tin (pan).

2 Put the instant coffee powder into a pan and stir in the milk, then add the sugar and set the pan over a medium-high heat. Bring to the boil, stirring constantly, until the coffee and sugar have dissolved.

3 Remove the pan from the heat and add the chocolate. Stir until the chocolate has melted and the sauce is smooth. Stir in the vanilla essence and coffee liqueur, if using.

4 In a bowl, whisk the egg yolks to blend them lightly. Slowly whisk in the chocolate mixture until well blended, then strain the mixture into a large jug and divide equally among the cups or ramekins in the roasting tin. Pour in enough boiling water to come halfway up the sides of the cups or ramekins. Cover the tin with foil.

5 Bake for 30–35 minutes until the custard is just set and a knife inserted into a custard comes out clean. Remove the cups or ramekins from the roasting tin and allow to cool. Place on a baking sheet, cover and chill completely. Decorate with the whipped cream and crystallized mimosa balls, if using.

Crème Brûlée

This dessert actually originated in Cambridge, England, but has become associated with France and is widely eaten there.

INGREDIENTS

Serves 6

1 vanilla pod (bean)
1 litre/1¾ pints/4 cups double (heavy) cream
6 egg yolks
90g/3½oz/½ cup caster (superfine) sugar
30ml/2 tbsp almond or orange liqueur (optional)
75g/3oz/⅓ cup soft light brown sugar

1 Preheat the oven to 150°C/300°F/Gas 2. Place six 120ml/4fl oz/½ cup ramekins in a roasting tin (pan) and set aside.

2 With a small sharp knife, split the vanilla pod lengthways and place it into a medium pan. Add the cream and bring just to the boil over a medium heat, stirring. Remove from the heat and cover. Set aside for 15–20 minutes, then remove the vanilla.

3 In a bowl, whisk the egg yolks, caster sugar and liqueur, if using, until well blended. Whisk in the hot cream and strain into a large jug. Divide the custard equally among the ramekins.

4 Pour enough boiling water into the roasting tin to come halfway up the sides of the ramekins. Cover the tin with foil and bake for about 30 minutes until the custards are just set. Remove from the tin and leave to cool. Return to the dry roasting tin and chill.

5 Preheat the grill (broiler). Sprinkle the sugar evenly over the surface of each custard and grill for 30–60 seconds until the sugar melts and caramelizes. (Do not let it burn or the custard curdle.) Place in the refrigerator to set the crust and serve chilled.

COOK'S TIP

To test if the custards are ready, push the point of a knife into the centre of one – if it comes out clean, the custards are cooked.

Crème Caramel

Crème caramel is one of the most popular French desserts and is wonderful when freshly made. This is a slightly lighter modern version of the traditional recipe.

INGREDIENTS

Serves 6–8

250g/9oz/1¼ cups granulated sugar

60ml/4 tbsp water

1 vanilla pod (bean) or 10ml/2 tsp vanilla essence (extract)

400ml/14fl oz/1⅔ cups milk

250ml/8fl oz/1 cup whipping cream

5 large (US extra large) eggs

2 egg yolks

1 Put 175g/6oz/⅞ cup of the sugar in a small heavy pan with 60ml/4 tbsp of water to moisten. Bring to the boil over a high heat, swirling the pan to dissolve the sugar. Boil, without stirring, until the syrup turns a dark caramel colour (this will take about 4–5 minutes).

2 Immediately pour the caramel into a 1 litre/1¾ pint/4 cup soufflé dish. Holding the dish with oven gloves, quickly swirl the dish to coat the base and sides with the caramel and set aside. (The caramel will harden quickly as it cools.)

3 Preheat the oven to 160°C/325°F/Gas 3. With a small sharp knife, carefully split the vanilla pod lengthways and scrape the black seeds into a medium saucepan. Add the milk and cream and bring just to the boil over a medium-high heat, stirring frequently. Remove the pan from the heat, cover and set aside for 15–20 minutes.

4 In a bowl, whisk the eggs and egg yolks with the remaining sugar for 2–3 minutes until smooth and creamy. Whisk in the hot milk and carefully strain the mixture into the caramel-lined dish. Cover with foil.

5 Place the dish in a roasting tin (pan) and pour in enough boiling water to come halfway up the sides of the dish. Bake the custard for 40–45 minutes until just set and a knife inserted about 5cm/2in from the edge comes out clean. Remove from the roasting tin and cool for at least 30 minutes, then chill overnight.

6 To turn out, carefully run a sharp knife around the edge of the dish to loosen the custard. Cover the dish with a serving plate and, holding them tightly, invert the dish and plate together. Gently lift one edge of the dish, allowing the caramel to run over the sides, then slowly lift off the dish.

HOT PUDDINGS

Magic Chocolate Mud Pudding

A popular favourite, which magically separates into a light and luscious sponge and a velvety chocolate sauce.

INGREDIENTS

Serves 4

50g/2oz/4 tbsp butter

200g/7oz/generous 1 cup light muscovado (molasses) sugar

475ml/16fl oz/2 cups milk

90g/3½oz/scant 1 cup self-raising flour

5ml/1 tsp ground cinnamon

75ml/5 tbsp cocoa powder

plain yogurt or vanilla ice cream, to serve

1 Preheat the oven to 180°C/350°F/Gas 4. Lightly grease a 1.5 litre/2½ pint/6 cup ovenproof dish and place on a baking sheet.

2 Place the butter in a heavy pan. Add 115g/4oz/¾ cup of the sugar and 150ml/¼ pint/⅔ cup of the milk. Heat gently, stirring from time to time, until the butter has melted and all the sugar has dissolved. Remove the pan from the heat.

3 Sift the flour, cinnamon and 15ml/1 tbsp of the cocoa powder into the pan and stir into the mixture, mixing evenly. Pour the mixture into the prepared dish and level the surface.

4 Sift the remaining sugar and cocoa powder into a bowl, mix well, then sprinkle over the pudding mixture.

5 Pour the remaining milk over the pudding.

6 Bake for 45–50 minutes or until the sponge has risen to the top and is firm to the touch. Serve hot, with the yogurt or vanilla ice cream.

COOK'S TIP

A soufflé dish will support the sponge as it rises above the sauce.

Hot Chocolate Zabaglione

A deliciously chocolate-flavoured variation of a classic Italian dessert.

INGREDIENTS

Serves 6

6 egg yolks
150g/5oz/¾ cup caster (superfine) sugar
45ml/3 tbsp cocoa powder
200ml/7fl oz/⅞ cup Marsala
cocoa powder or icing (confectioners') sugar, for dusting
almond biscuits or cookies, to serve

1 Half fill a medium pan with water and bring to simmering point.

2 Place the egg yolks and sugar in a heatproof bowl and whisk until the mixture is pale and all the sugar has dissolved.

3 Add the cocoa and Marsala, then place the bowl over the simmering water. Whisk until the consistency of the mixture is smooth, thick and foamy.

4 Pour quickly into tall heatproof glasses, dust lightly with cocoa or icing sugar and serve immediately with almond biscuits.

Pears in Chocolate Fudge Blankets

Warm poached pears coated in a chocolate fudge sauce – irresistible.

INGREDIENTS

Serves 6

6 ripe eating pears
30ml/2 tbsp lemon juice
75g/3oz/scant ½ cup caster (superfine) sugar
1 cinnamon stick

For the sauce
200ml/7fl oz/⅞ cup double (heavy) cream
150g/5oz/scant 1 cup light muscovado (molasses) sugar
25g/1oz/2 tbsp unsalted butter
60ml/4 tbsp golden (light corn) syrup
120ml/4fl oz/½ cup milk
200g/7oz plain (semisweet) dark chocolate, broken into squares

1 Peel the pears thinly, leaving the stalks on. Scoop out the cores from the base. Brush the cut surfaces with lemon juice to prevent browning.

2 Place the sugar and 300ml/½ pint/1¼ cups of water in a large saucepan. Heat gently until the sugar dissolves. Add the pears and cinnamon stick with any remaining lemon juice, and, if necessary, a little more water, so that the pears are almost covered.

3 Bring to the boil, then lower the heat, cover the pan and simmer the pears gently for 15–20 minutes.

4 Meanwhile, make the sauce. Place the cream, sugar, butter, golden syrup and milk in a heavy pan. Heat gently until the sugar has dissolved and the butter and syrup have melted, then bring to the boil. Boil, stirring constantly, for about 5 minutes or until thick and smooth.

5 Remove the pan from the heat and stir in the chocolate, a little at a time, until melted.

6 Using a slotted spoon, transfer the poached pears to a dish. Keep hot. Boil the syrup rapidly to reduce to about 45–60ml/3–4 tbsp. Remove the cinnamon stick and gently stir the syrup into the chocolate sauce.

7 Serve the pears in individual bowls or on dessert plates, with the hot chocolate fudge sauce spooned over them.

Chocolate Soufflé Crêpes

A non-stick pan is ideal as it does not need greasing between each crêpe. Serve two crêpes per person.

INGREDIENTS

Makes 12 crêpes

75g/3oz/⅔ cup plain (all-purpose) flour
10g/¼oz/1 tbsp unsweetened cocoa
5ml/1 tsp caster (superfine) sugar
pinch of salt
5ml/1 tsp ground cinnamon
2 eggs
175ml/6fl oz/¾ cup milk
5ml/1 tsp vanilla essence (extract)
50g/2oz/4 tbsp unsalted butter, melted
icing (confectioners') sugar, for dusting
raspberries, pineapple and mint sprigs, to decorate

For the pineapple syrup

½ medium pineapple, peeled, cored and finely chopped
30ml/2 tbsp natural maple syrup
5ml/1 tsp cornflour (cornstarch)
½ cinnamon stick
30ml/2 tbsp rum

For the soufflé filling

250g/9oz semi-sweet or bittersweet chocolate
85ml/3fl oz/⅓ cup double (heavy) cream
3 eggs, separated
25g/1oz/2 tbsp caster sugar

1 Prepare the syrup. In a pan over medium heat, bring the pineapple, 125ml/4fl oz/½ cup of water, maple syrup, cornflour and cinnamon stick to the boil. Simmer for 2–3 minutes until the sauce thickens, whisking frequently. Remove from the heat; discard the cinnamon. Pour into a bowl, stir in the rum and chill.

2 Prepare the crêpes. In a bowl, sift the flour, cocoa, sugar, salt and cinnamon. Stir to blend, then make a well in the centre. In a bowl, beat the eggs, milk and vanilla. Gradually add to the well, whisking in flour to form a smooth batter. Stir in half the melted butter and pour the batter into a jug. Let stand for 1 hour.

3 Heat an 18–20cm/7–8in crêpe pan. Brush with butter. Stir the batter. Pour 45ml/3 tbsp batter into the pan; swirl the pan quickly to cover the bottom with a thin layer. Cook over medium-high heat for 1–2 minutes until the bottom is golden. Turn over and cook for 30–45 seconds. Turn on to a plate and stack between non-stick baking paper.

4 Prepare the filling. In a small pan, over medium heat, melt the chocolate and cream until smooth, stirring frequently.

5 In a bowl, beat the yolks with half the sugar until light and creamy. Gradually beat in the chocolate mixture. Allow to cool. In a large bowl, beat the egg whites until soft peaks form. Gradually beat in the remaining sugar until stiff. Beat in a spoonful of egg whites to the chocolate mixture, then fold in the remaining whites.

6 Preheat the oven to 200°C/400°F/Gas 6. Lay a crêpe on a plate. Spoon a little soufflé mixture on to the crêpe, spreading it to the edge. Fold the bottom half over the soufflé mixture, then fold in half again to form a filled 'triangle'. Place on a buttered baking sheet. Repeat with the remaining crêpes.

7 Brush the tops with melted butter and bake for 15–20 minutes until filling has souffléd. Dust with icing sugar and garnish with raspberries, pineapple, mint and a spoonful of pineapple syrup.

Baked Apples with Apricot Filling

An alternative stuffing mixture for baked apples, with a refreshing fruit flavour.

INGREDIENTS

Serves 6

75g/3oz/scant ½ cup chopped, ready-to-eat dried apricots
50g/2oz/½ cup chopped walnuts
5ml/1 tsp grated lemon rind
2.5ml/½ tsp ground cinnamon
90g/3½oz/½ cup soft light brown sugar
25g/1oz/2 tbsp butter, at room temperature
6 large eating apples
15ml/1 tbsp melted butter

1 Preheat the oven to 190°C/375°F/Gas 5. Place the apricots, walnuts, lemon rind and cinnamon in a bowl. Add the sugar and butter and stir until thoroughly mixed.

2 Core the apples, without cutting all the way through to the base. Peel the top of each apple and then slightly widen the top of each opening to make room for the filling.

3 Spoon the filling into the apples, packing it down lightly.

4 Place the stuffed apples in an ovenproof dish large enough to hold them all comfortably side by side.

5 Brush the apples with the melted butter. Bake for 45–50 minutes, until they are tender. Serve hot.

COOK'S TIP

Accompany with real custard, Crème Anglaise, made using cream, egg yolks, caster (superfine) sugar and a few drops of vanilla essence (extract).

Apple Soufflé Omelette

Apples sautéed until they are slightly caramelized make a delicious filling – you could use fresh raspberries or strawberries when they are in season.

INGREDIENTS

Serves 2

4 eggs, separated
30ml/2 tbsp single (light) cream
15ml/1 tbsp caster (superfine) sugar
15g/½oz/1 tbsp butter
icing (confectioners') sugar, for dredging

For the filling
1 eating apple, peeled, cored and sliced
25g/1oz/2 tbsp butter
30ml/2 tbsp soft light brown sugar
45ml/3 tbsp single cream

1 To make the filling, sauté the apple slices in the butter and sugar until just tender. Stir in the cream and keep warm, while making the omelette.

2 Place the egg yolks in a bowl with the cream and sugar and beat well. Whisk the egg whites until they form stiff peaks, then fold into the yolk mixture.

3 Melt the butter in a large heavy frying pan, pour in the soufflé mixture and spread evenly. Cook for 1 minute until golden underneath, then cover the pan handle with foil and place under a hot grill (broiler) to brown the top.

4 Slide the omelette on to a plate, add the apple mixture, then fold over. Sift the icing sugar over thickly, then mark in a criss-cross pattern with a hot metal skewer. Serve immediately.

Blackberry Cobbler

Make the most of the fresh autumn blackberries with this juicy dessert.

INGREDIENTS

Serves 8

800g/1¾lb/6 cups blackberries
200g/7oz/1 cup granulated sugar
20g/¾oz/3 tbsp plain (all-purpose) flour
grated rind of 1 lemon
30ml/2 tbsp granulated sugar mixed with
   1.5ml/¼ tsp grated nutmeg

For the topping
225g/8oz/2 cups plain flour
200g/7oz/1 cup granulated sugar
15ml/1 tbsp baking powder
pinch of salt
250ml/8fl oz/1 cup milk
115g/4oz/½ cup butter, melted

1 Preheat the oven to 180°C/350°F/Gas 4. In a bowl, combine the blackberries, sugar, flour and lemon rind. Stir gently to blend. Transfer to a 2.4 litre/4 pint baking dish.

2 For the topping, sift the flour, sugar, baking powder and salt into a large bowl. In a large jug, combine the milk and butter.

3 Gradually stir the milk mixture into the dry ingredients and stir until the batter is just smooth.

4 Spoon the batter over the berries, spreading to the edges.

5 Sprinkle the surface with the sugar and nutmeg mixture. Bake until the batter topping is set and lightly browned, about 50 minutes. Serve hot.

COOK'S TIP

If liked, use half blackberries and half raspberries or strawberries for the filling.

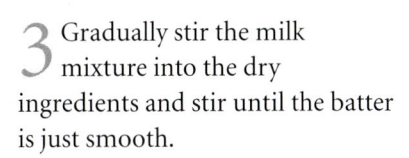

Apple Brown Betty

This simple dessert tastes good with cream or ice cream.

INGREDIENTS

Serves 6

50g/2oz/1 cup fresh breadcrumbs
50g/2oz/¾ cup soft light brown sugar, firmly packed
2.5ml/½ tsp ground cinnamon
1.5ml/¼ tsp ground cloves
1.5ml/¼ tsp grated nutmeg
50g/2oz/4 tbsp butter
900g/2lb tart-sweet apples
juice of 1 lemon
50g/2oz/⅓ cup finely chopped walnuts

1 Preheat the grill (broiler). Spread the breadcrumbs on a baking sheet and toast under the grill until golden, stirring so they colour evenly. Set aside.

2 Preheat the oven to 190°C/375°F/Gas 5. Butter a 2.4 litre/4 pint baking dish. Set aside.

3 Mix the sugar with the spices. Cut the butter into pea-size pieces. Set aside.

4 Peel, core and slice the apples. Toss immediately with the lemon juice to prevent the apple slices from turning brown.

5 Sprinkle about 40ml/2½ tbsp of breadcrumbs over the bottom of the prepared dish. Cover with a third of the apple slices and sprinkle with a third of the sugar-spice mixture. Add another layer of breadcrumbs and dot with a third of the butter. Repeat the layers two more times, ending with a layer of breadcrumbs. Sprinkle with the nuts, and dot with the remaining butter.

6 Bake until the apples are tender and the top is golden brown, 35–40 minutes. Serve hot or warm.

Spiced Peach Crumble

The topping of this classic dessert has rolled oats added for extra crunchiness.

INGREDIENTS

Serves 6

1.5kg/3lb ripe but firm peaches, peeled, stoned (pitted) and sliced
60ml/4 tbsp caster (superfine) sugar
2.5ml/½ tsp ground cinnamon
5ml/1 tsp lemon juice
whipped cream or vanilla ice cream, for serving (optional)

For the topping
115g/4oz/1 cup plain (all-purpose) flour
1.5ml/¼ tsp ground cinnamon
1.5ml/¼ tsp ground allspice
75g/3oz/1 cup rolled oats
175g/6oz/¾ cup soft light brown sugar
115g/4oz/8 tbsp butter

1 Preheat the oven to 190°C/375°F/Gas 5. For the topping, sift the flour and spices into a bowl. Add the oats and sugar and stir to combine. Cut or rub in the butter until the mixture resembles coarse crumbs.

2 Toss the peaches with the sugar, cinnamon and lemon juice. Put the fruit mixture in a 20–23cm/8–9in diameter baking dish.

3 Scatter the topping over the fruit in an even layer. Bake for 30–35 minutes. Serve warm, with whipped cream or vanilla ice cream, if liked.

VARIATION

Use apricots or nectarines instead of peaches. Substitute nutmeg for the cinnamon.

Apricot and Pear Filo Roulade

This is a very quick way of making a strudel – normally, very time consuming to do – and it tastes delicious!

INGREDIENTS

Serves 4–6

115g/4oz/½ cup ready-to-eat dried apricots, chopped
30ml/2 tbsp apricot jam
5ml/1 tsp lemon juice
50g/2oz/¼ cup soft (light) brown sugar
2 medium pears, peeled, cored and chopped
50g/2oz/½ cup ground almonds
30ml/2 tbsp flaked (sliced) almonds
25g/1oz/2 tbsp butter
8 sheets filo pastry
icing (confectioners') sugar, to dust

1 Put the apricots, apricot jam, lemon juice, brown sugar and pears into a pan and heat gently, stirring, for 5–7 minutes.

2 Remove from the heat and cool. Mix in the ground and flaked almonds. Preheat the oven to 200°C/400°F/Gas 6. Melt the butter in a pan.

3 Lightly grease a baking sheet. Layer the pastry on the baking sheet, brushing each layer with the melted butter.

4 Spoon the filling down the pastry just to one side of the centre and within 2.5cm/1in of each end. Lift the other side of the pastry up by sliding a palette knife underneath.

5 Fold this pastry over the filling, tucking the edge under. Seal the ends neatly and brush all over with butter again.

6 Bake for 15–20 minutes, until golden. Dust with icing sugar and serve hot.

American Spiced Pumpkin Pie

The unofficial national dish of the United States.

INGREDIENTS

Serves 4–6

175g/6oz/1½ cups plain (all-purpose) flour
pinch of salt
75g/3oz/6 tbsp unsalted butter
15ml/1 tbsp caster (superfine) sugar
450g/1lb/4 cups peeled fresh pumpkin, cubed, or 400g/14oz/2 cups canned pumpkin, drained
115g/4oz/½ cup soft light brown sugar
1.5ml/¼ tsp salt
1.5ml/¼ ground allspice
2.5ml/½ tsp ground cinnamon
2.5ml/½ tsp ground ginger
2 eggs, lightly beaten
120ml/4fl oz/½ cup double (heavy) cream
whipped cream, to serve

1 Place the flour in a bowl with the salt and butter and rub with your fingertips until the mixture resembles breadcrumbs (or use a food processor).

2 Stir in the caster sugar, add about 30–45ml/2–3 tbsp water and mix to a soft dough. Knead the dough lightly on a floured surface. Flatten out into a round, wrap in a plastic bag and chill for 1 hour.

3 Preheat the oven to 200°C/400°F/Gas 6 with a baking sheet inside. If you are using raw pumpkin for the pie, steam for 15 minutes until quite tender, then leave to cool completely. Purée the steamed or canned pumpkin in a food processor or blender until it is very smooth.

4 Roll out the pastry quite thinly and use to line a 24cm/9½in (measured across the top) x 2.5cm/1in deep pie tin. Trim off any excess pastry and reserve for the decoration. Prick the base of the pastry case with a fork.

5 Cut as many leaf shapes as you can from the excess pastry and make vein markings with the back of a knife on each. Brush the edge of the pastry with water and stick the leaves all round the edge. Chill.

6 In a large bowl mix together the pumpkin purée, brown sugar, salt, spices, eggs and cream and pour into the prepared pastry case. Smooth the top with a knife.

7 Place on the preheated baking sheet and bake for 15 minutes. Then reduce the temperature to 180°C/350°F/Gas 4 and cook for a further 30 minutes, or until the filling is set and the pastry golden. Serve the pie warm with a generous dollop of whipped cream.

Cabinet Pudding

A rich, baked custard, flavoured with glacé and dried fruit.

INGREDIENTS

Serves 4

25g/1oz/2½ tbsp raisins, chopped
30ml/2 tbsp brandy (optional)
25g/1oz/2½ tbsp glacé (candied) cherries, halved
25g/1oz/2½ tbsp angelica, chopped
2 trifle sponge cakes, diced
50g/2oz ratafias (macaroons), crushed
2 eggs
2 egg yolks
30ml/2 tbsp sugar
450ml/¾ pint/1⅞ cups single (light) cream or milk
few drops of vanilla essence (extract)

1 Soak the raisins in the brandy, if using, for several hours.

2 Butter a 750ml/1¼ pint/3 cup charlotte mould and arrange some of the cherries and angelica in the base.

3 Mix the remaining cherries and angelica with the sponge cakes, ratafias and raisins and brandy, if using, and spoon into the mould.

4 Lightly whisk together the eggs, egg yolks and sugar. Bring the cream or milk just to the boil, then stir into the egg mixture with the vanilla essence.

5 Strain the egg mixture into the mould, then leave for 15–30 minutes.

6 Preheat the oven to 160°C/325°F/Gas 3. Place the mould in a roasting tin (pan), cover with baking parchment and pour in boiling water to come halfway up the side of the mould. Bake for 1 hour, or until set. Leave for 2–3 minutes, then turn out on to a warm plate, to serve.

Eve's Pudding

The tempting apples beneath the sponge topping are the reason for the pudding's name.

INGREDIENTS

Serves 4–6

115g/4oz/½ cup butter
115g/4oz/generous ½ cup caster (superfine) sugar
2 eggs, beaten
grated rind and juice of 1 lemon
90g/3½oz/scant 1 cup self-raising flour
40g/1½oz/⅓ cup ground almonds
115g/4oz/scant ½ cup soft (light) brown sugar
675g/1½lb cooking apples, cored and thinly sliced
25g/1oz/¼ cup flaked (sliced) almonds
whipped cream, to serve (optional)

1 Beat together the butter and caster sugar in a large mixing bowl until the mixture is very light and fluffy.

2 Gradually beat the eggs into the butter mixture, beating well after each addition, then fold in the lemon rind, flour and ground almonds.

3 Mix the brown sugar, apples and lemon juice, tip into the dish, add the sponge mixture, then the almonds. Bake for 40–45 minutes, until golden. Serve hot, with cream, if liked.

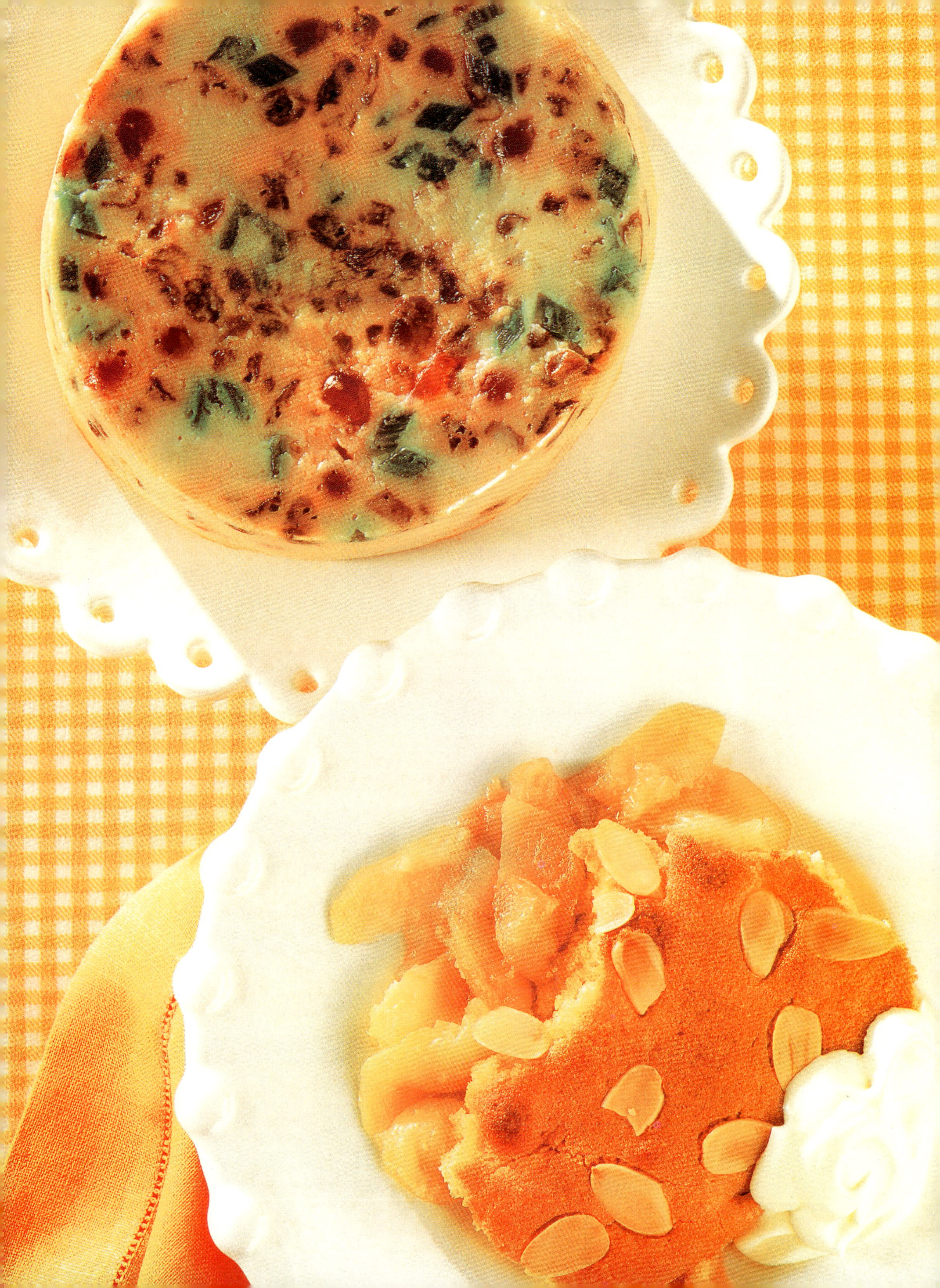

Christmas Pudding

This recipe makes enough to fill one 1.2 litre/2 pint/5 cup bowl or two 600ml/1 pint/2½ cup bowls. It can be made up to a month before Christmas and stored in a cool, dry place. Serve the pudding with brandy or rum butter, whisky sauce, custard or whipped cream.

INGREDIENTS

Serves 8

115g/4oz/½ cup butter

225g/8oz/1 rounded cup soft dark brown sugar

50g/2oz/½ cup self-raising flour

5ml/1tsp ground mixed (pumpkin pie) spice

1.5ml/¼ tsp grated nutmeg

2.5ml/½ tsp ground cinnamon

2 eggs

115g/4oz/2 cups fresh white breadcrumbs

175g/6oz/generous 1 cup sultanas (golden raisins)

175g/6oz/generous 1 cup raisins

115g/4oz/½ cup currants

25g/1oz/3 tbsp mixed candied peel, chopped finely

25g/1oz/¼ cup chopped almonds

1 small cooking apple, peeled, cored and coarsely grated

finely grated rind of 1 orange or lemon

juice of 1 orange or lemon, made up to 150ml/¼ pint/⅔ cup with brandy, rum or sherry

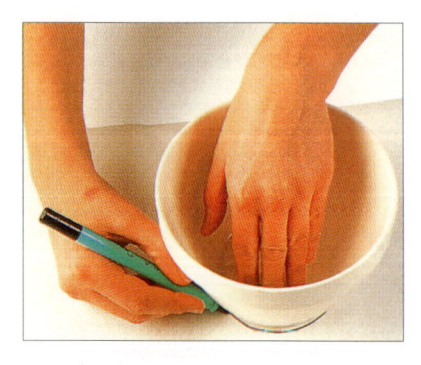

1 Cut a disc of greaseproof (waxed) paper to fit the base of the bowl(s) and butter the disc and bowl(s).

2 Whisk the butter and sugar together until soft. Beat in the flour, spices and eggs. Stir in the remaining ingredients thoroughly. The mixture should have a soft dropping consistency.

3 Turn the mixture into the greased bowl(s) and level the top with a spoon.

4 Cover with another disc of buttered greaseproof paper.

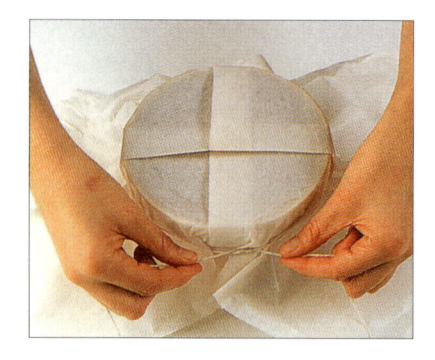

5 Make two pleats across the centre of a large piece of greaseproof paper and cover the bowl(s) with it, tying it in place with string under the rim. Cut off the excess paper. Pleat a piece of foil in the same way and cover the bowl(s) with it, tucking it around the bowl neatly, under the greaseproof frill. Tie another piece of string around and across the top, as a handle.

6 Place the bowl(s) in a steamer over a pan of simmering water and steam for 6 hours. Alternatively, put the bowl(s) into a large pan and pour round enough boiling water to come halfway up the bowl(s) and cover the pan with a tight-fitting lid. Check the water is simmering and top it up with boiling water as it evaporates. When the pudding(s) have cooked, leave to cool completely. Then remove the foil and greaseproof paper. Wipe the bowl(s) clean and replace the greaseproof paper and foil with clean pieces, ready for reheating.

TO SERVE

Steam for 2 hours. Turn on to a plate and leave to stand for 5 minutes, before removing the pudding bowl (the steam will rise to the top of the bowl and help to loosen the pudding). Decorate with a sprig of holly.

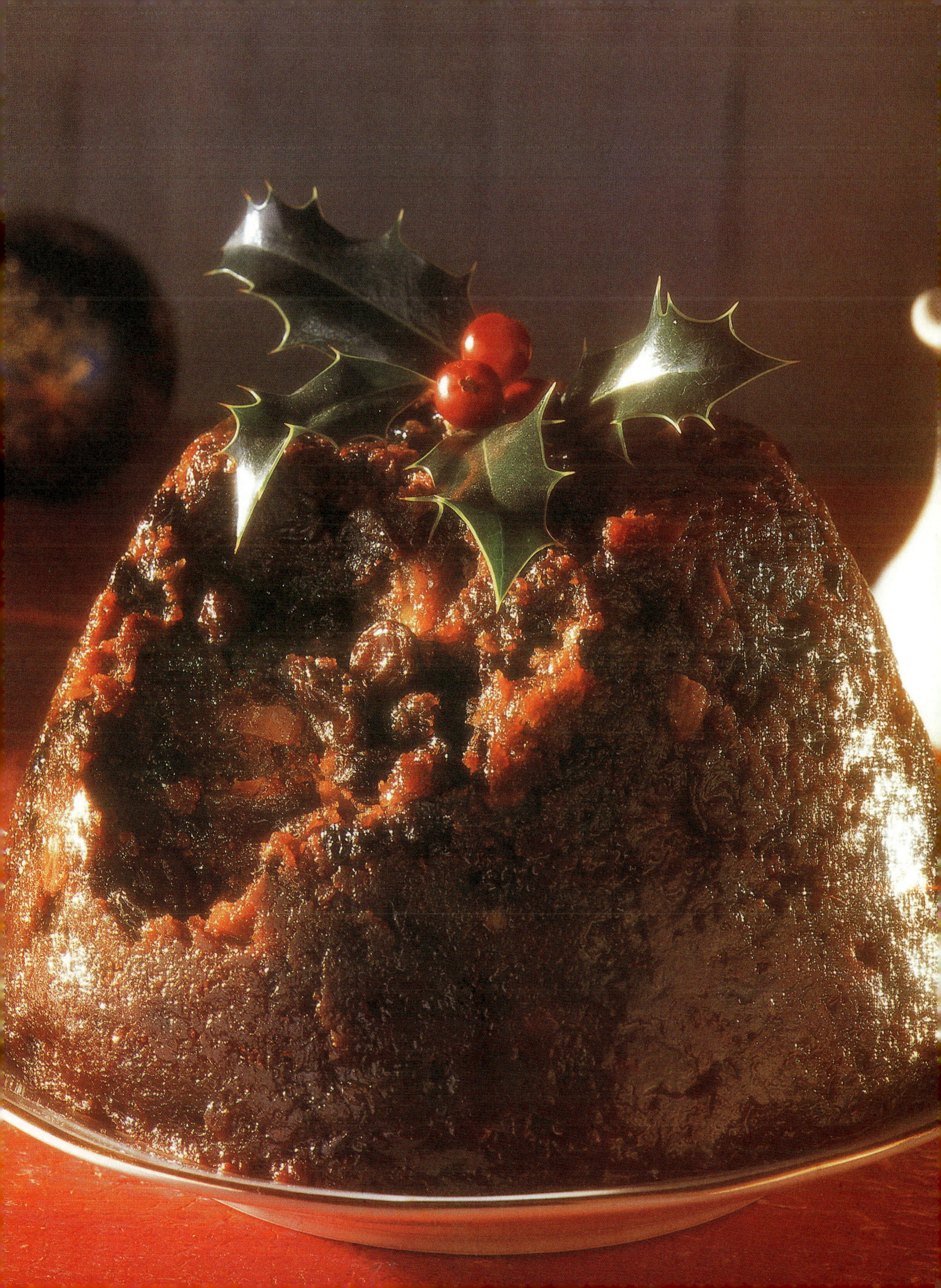

Vermont Baked Maple Custard

Use pure maple syrup if you can for this custard as it will really enhance the flavour.

INGREDIENTS

Serves 6

3 eggs
120ml/4fl oz/½ cup maple syrup
600ml/1 pint/2½ cups milk
pinch of salt
pinch of grated nutmeg

COOK'S TIP

Baking delicate mixtures such as custards in a water bath helps protect them from uneven heating which could make them rubbery.

1 Preheat the oven to 180°C/350°F/Gas 4. Combine all the ingredients in a large bowl and mix together thoroughly.

2 Set individual custard cups or ramekins in a roasting tin (pan) half filled with hot water. Pour the custard mixture into the cups. Bake until the custards are set, 45 minutes–1 hour. Test by inserting the blade of a knife in the centre: it should come out clean. Serve warm.

Bread Pudding with Pecan Nuts

A version of the British classic deliciously flavoured with pecan nuts and orange rind.

INGREDIENTS

Serves 6

400ml/14fl oz/1⅔ cups milk
400ml/14fl oz/1⅔ cups single (light) or whipping cream
150g/5oz/¾ cup caster (superfine) sugar
3 eggs, beaten to mix
10ml/2 tsp grated orange rind
5ml/1 tsp vanilla essence (extract)
24 slices of day-old French bread, 1.5cm/½in thick
75g/3oz/½ cup toasted pecan nuts, chopped
icing (confectioners') sugar, for sprinkling
whipped cream or sour cream and maple syrup, to serve

1 Put 350ml/12fl oz/1½ cups each of the milk and cream in a pan. Add the sugar. Warm over low heat, stirring to dissolve the sugar. Remove from the heat and cool. Add the eggs, orange rind and vanilla and mix well.

2 Arrange half of the bread slices in a buttered 23–25cm/9–10in baking dish. Scatter two-thirds of the pecans over the bread. Arrange the remaining bread slices on top and scatter on the rest of the pecans.

3 Pour the egg mixture evenly over the bread slices. Soak for 30 minutes. Press the top layer of bread down into the liquid once or twice.

4 Preheat the oven to 180°C/350°F/Gas 4. If the top layer of bread slices looks dry and all the liquid has been absorbed, moisten with the remaining milk and cream.

5 Set the baking dish in a roasting tin (pan). Add enough water to the tin to come halfway up the sides of the dish. Bring the water to the boil.

6 Transfer to the oven. Bake for 40 minutes or until the pudding is set and golden brown on top. Sprinkle the top of the pudding with sifted icing sugar and serve warm, with whipped cream or sour cream and maple syrup, if you like.

Quick and Easy

Frudités with Honey Dip

A colourful and tasty variation on the popular savoury crudités.

INGREDIENTS

Serves 4

225g/8oz/1 cup Greek (US strained plain) yogurt

45ml/3 tbsp clear honey

selection of fresh fruit for dipping such as apples, pears, tangerines, grapes, figs, cherries, strawberries and kiwi fruit

1 Place the yogurt in a dish, beat until smooth, then partially stir in the honey, leaving an attractive marbled effect.

2 Cut the various fruits into wedges or bite-sized pieces or leave whole.

3 Arrange the fruits on a platter with the bowl of dip in the centre. Serve chilled.

COOK'S TIP

Sprinkle the apple and pear wedges with lemon juice to prevent discolouring.

Yogurt with Apricots and Pistachios

If you allow a thick yogurt to drain overnight, it becomes even thicker and more luscious. Add honeyed apricots and nuts and you have an exotic yet simple dessert.

INGREDIENTS

Serves 4

450g/1lb Greek (US strained plain) yogurt
175g/6oz/⅔ cup ready-to-eat dried apricots, chopped
15ml/1 tbsp clear honey
grated rind of 1 orange
30ml/2 tbsp unsalted pistachios, roughly chopped
ground cinnamon

1 Place the yogurt in a fine sieve over a bowl, and allow it to drain overnight in the refrigerator.

2 Discard the whey from the yogurt. Place the apricots in a pan, barely cover with water and simmer for just 3 minutes, to soften. Drain and cool, then mix with the honey.

3 Mix the yogurt with the apricots, orange rind and nuts. Spoon into sundae dishes, sprinkle over a little cinnamon and chill.

VARIATION

For a simple dessert, strain the fruit, cover with yogurt and sprinkle with demerara (raw) sugar and a little ginger or cinnamon.

Fresh Pineapple Salad

Very refreshing, this salad can be prepared ahead. Orange flower water is available from Middle Eastern food stores or good delicatessens.

INGREDIENTS

Serves 4

1 small ripe pineapple
icing (confectioners') sugar, to taste
15ml/1 tbsp orange flower water, or more if liked
115g/4oz/good ½ cup fresh dates, stoned (pitted) and quartered
225g/8oz fresh strawberries, sliced
few fresh mint sprigs, to decorate

1 Cut the skin from the pineapple and, using the tip of a vegetable peeler, remove as many brown "eyes" as possible. Quarter lengthways, remove the core, then slice.

2 Lay the pineapple in a shallow glass bowl. Sprinkle with sugar and orange flower water.

3 Add the dates and strawberries to the pineapple, cover and chill for at least 2 hours, stirring once or twice. Serve lightly chilled decorated with a few mint sprigs.

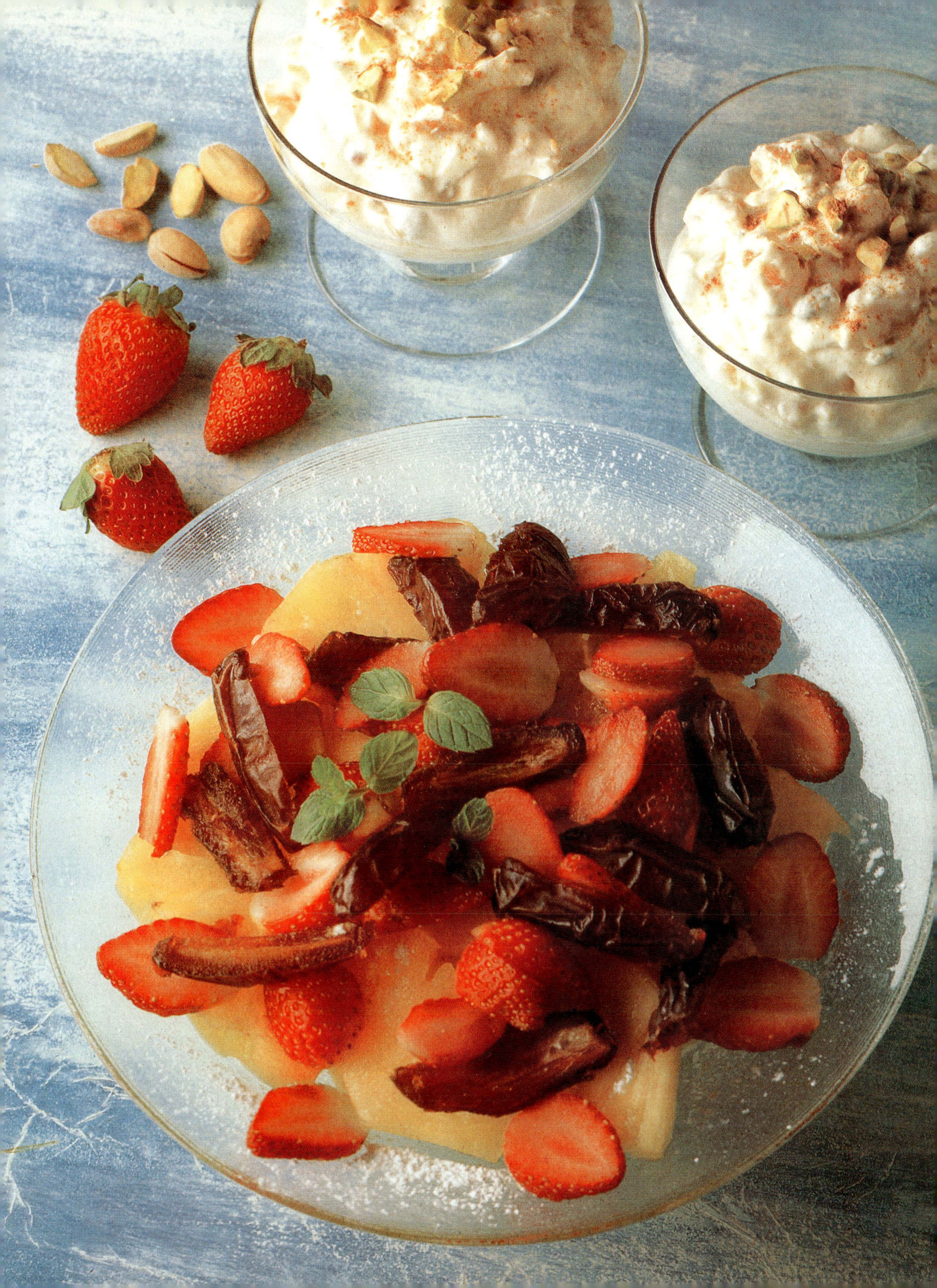

Prune and Orange Pots

A simple dessert, made in minutes, that can be served straight away, but is best chilled before serving.

INGREDIENTS

Serves 4

225g/8oz/1 cup ready-to-eat dried prunes
150ml/¼ pint/⅔ cup orange juice
225g/8oz/1 cup low-fat natural (plain) yogurt
shreds of orange rind, to decorate

1 Roughly chop the prunes and place them in a pan with the orange juice.

2 Bring the juice to the boil, stirring. Reduce the heat, cover and leave to simmer for 5 minutes, until the prunes are tender and the liquid is reduced by half.

3 Remove from the heat, allow to cool slightly and then beat well with a wooden spoon, until the fruit breaks down to a rough purée.

4 Transfer the mixture to a bowl. Stir in the yogurt, swirling the yogurt and fruit purée together lightly, to give an attractive marbled effect.

5 Spoon the mixture into stemmed glasses or individual dishes, smoothing the tops.

6 Top each dish with a few shreds of orange rind, to decorate. Chill before serving.

VARIATION

This dessert can also be made with other ready-to-eat dried fruit, such as apricots or peaches. For a special occasion, add a dash of brandy or Cointreau with the yogurt.

Quick Apricot Blender Whip

One of the quickest desserts you can make – and one of the prettiest.

INGREDIENTS

Serves 4

400g/14oz can apricot halves in juice
15ml/1 tbsp Grand Marnier or brandy
175g/6oz/¾ cup Greek (US strained plain) yogurt
30ml/2 tbsp flaked (sliced) almonds

1 Drain the juice from the apricots and place the fruit and liqueur in a blender or food processor.

2 Process the apricots to a smooth purée.

3 Spoon the fruit purée and yogurt in alternate spoonfuls into four tall glasses or glass dishes, swirling them together slightly to give a marbled effect.

4 Lightly toast the almonds until they are golden. Let them cool and then sprinkle them over the top.

COOK'S TIP

For an even lighter dessert, use low-fat instead of Greek (whole-fat) yogurt, and a little fruit juice from the can instead of liqueur.

Almost Instant Banana Pudding

Banana and ginger make a great combination in this very fast dessert.

INGREDIENTS

Serves 6–8

4 thick slices ginger cake or gingerbread
6 bananas
30ml/2 tbsp lemon juice
300ml/½ pint/1¼ cups whipping cream or fromage frais
60ml/4 tbsp fruit juice
30–45ml/3–4 tbsp soft (light) brown sugar

1 Break up the cake into chunks and arrange in an ovenproof dish. Slice the bananas and toss in the lemon juice.

2 Whip the cream and, when firm, gently whip in the juice. (If using fromage frais, just gently stir in the juice.) Fold in the bananas and spoon the mixture over the ginger cake.

3 Top with the soft brown sugar and place under a hot grill (broiler) for 2–3 minutes to caramelize. Chill to set firm again if you wish.

Ginger and Orange Crème Brûlée

This is a useful way of cheating at crème brûlée!

INGREDIENTS

Serves 4–5

2 eggs, plus 2 egg yolks
300ml/½ pint/1¼ cups single (light) cream
30ml/2 tbsp caster (superfine) sugar
5ml/1 tsp powdered gelatine or alternative
finely grated rind and juice of ½ orange
1 large piece stem (preserved) ginger, finely chopped
45–60ml/3–4 tbsp icing (confectioners') or caster sugar
orange segments and sprig of mint, to decorate

1 Whisk the eggs and yolks together until pale. Bring the cream and sugar to the boil, remove from the heat and sprinkle on the gelatine. Stir until the gelatine has dissolved and then pour the cream mixture on to the eggs, whisking all the time.

2 Add the orange rind, a little juice to taste, and the chopped ginger to the mixture.

3 Pour into four or five ramekins and chill until set.

4 Before serving, sprinkle the sugar generously over the top of the custard and put under a very hot grill (broiler). Watch closely for the couple of moments it takes for the tops to caramelize. Allow to cool before serving. Decorate with a few segments of orange and a sprig of mint.

COOK'S TIP

For a milder ginger flavour, just add up to 5ml/1 tsp ground ginger instead of the stem ginger.

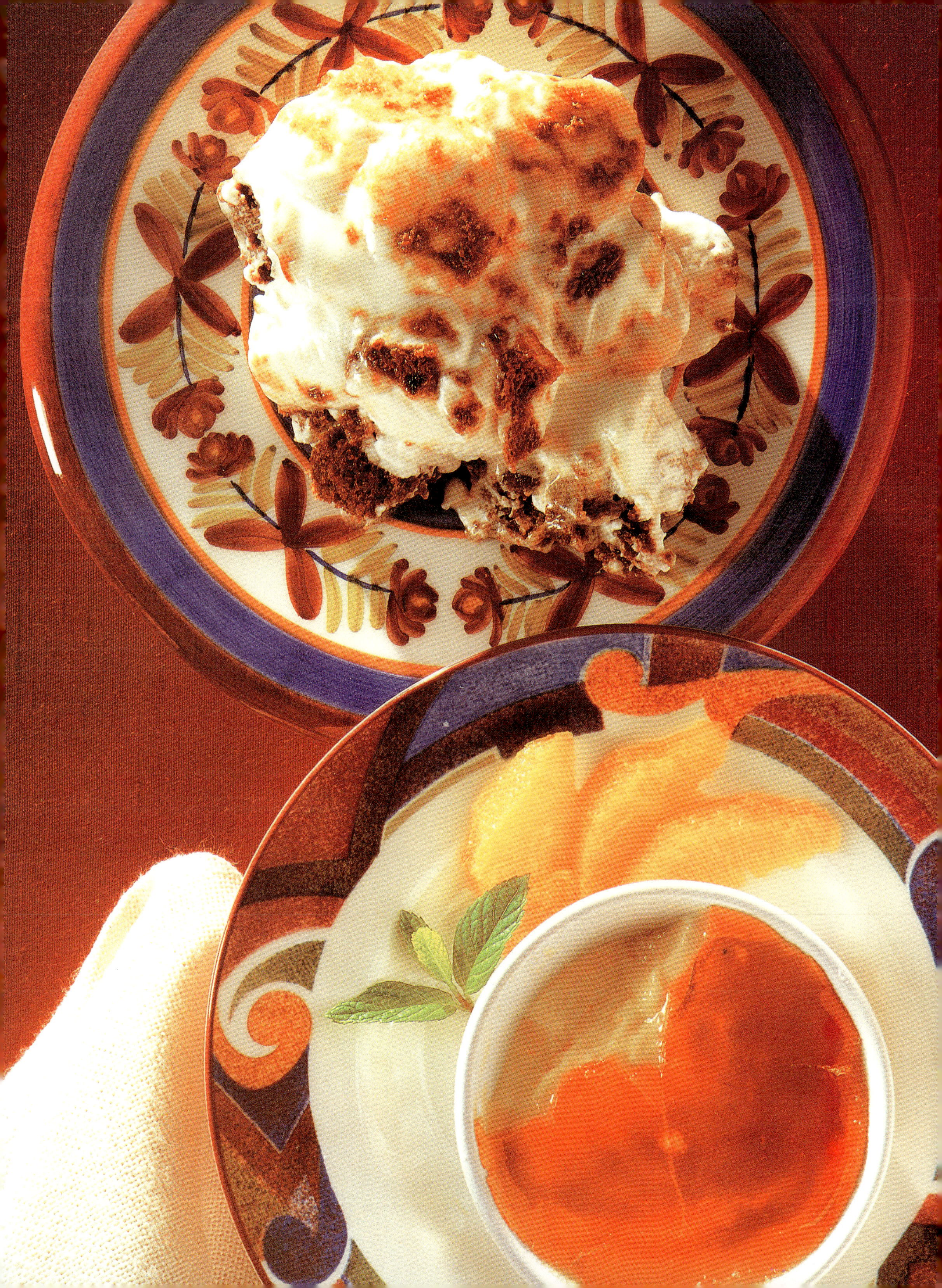

Chocolate Fudge Sundaes

INGREDIENTS

Serves 4

4 scoops each vanilla and coffee ice cream
2 small ripe bananas, sliced
whipped cream
toasted flaked (sliced) almonds

For the sauce

50g/2oz/¼ cup soft light brown sugar
120ml/4fl oz/½ cup golden (light corn) syrup
45ml/3 tbsp strong black coffee
5ml/1 tsp ground cinnamon
150g/5oz plain (semisweet) chocolate, chopped
85ml/3fl oz/⅓ cup whipping cream
45ml/3 tbsp coffee liqueur (optional)

1 To make the sauce, place the sugar, syrup, coffee and cinnamon in a heavy pan. Bring to the boil, then boil for about 5 minutes, stirring the mixture constantly.

2 Turn off the heat and stir in the chocolate. When melted and smooth, stir in the cream and liqueur, if using. Leave the sauce to cool slightly. If made ahead, reheat the sauce gently until just warm.

3 Fill four glasses with one scoop of vanilla and another of coffee ice cream.

4 Sprinkle the sliced bananas over the ice cream. Pour the warm fudge sauce over the bananas, then top each sundae with a generous swirl of whipped cream. Sprinkle with toasted almonds and serve immediately.

VARIATION

Try using other flavours of ice cream, such as strawberry, praline or chocolate. In the summer, use raspberries or strawberries in place of bananas, and sprinkle chopped roasted hazelnuts on top in place of the flaked almonds.

Brazilian Coffee Bananas

Rich, and sinful-looking, this dessert takes only two minutes to make!

INGREDIENTS

Serves 4

4 small ripe bananas

15ml/1 tbsp instant coffee powder

30ml/2 tbsp dark muscovado (molasses) sugar

250g/9oz/1⅛ cups Greek (US strained plain) yogurt

15ml/1 tbsp toasted flaked (sliced) almonds

1 Peel and slice one banana and mash the remaining three with a fork.

2 Dissolve the coffee in 15ml/1 tbsp of hot water and stir into the mashed bananas.

3 Spoon a little of the mashed banana mixture into four serving dishes and sprinkle with sugar. Top with a spoonful of yogurt, then repeat until all the ingredients are used up.

4 Swirl the last layer of yogurt for a marbled effect. Finish with a few banana slices and flaked almonds. Serve cold. Best eaten within about an hour of making.

VARIATION

For a special occasion, add a dash of dark rum or brandy to the bananas for extra richness.

Low Calorie

Fruited Rice Ring

This beautiful dessert makes a perfect centrepiece for a light lunch.

INGREDIENTS

Serves 4

65g/2½oz/5 tbsp short grain rice
900ml/1½ pint/3¾ cups semi-skimmed (low-fat) milk
1 cinnamon stick
175g/6oz/1 cup mixed dried fruit
175ml/6fl oz/¾ cup orange juice
45ml/3 tbsp caster (superfine) sugar
finely grated rind of 1 small orange

1 Place the rice, milk and cinnamon stick in a large pan and bring to the boil. Cover and simmer, stirring occasionally, for about 1½ hours, until no free liquid remains.

2 Meanwhile, place the fruit and orange juice in a pan and bring to the boil. Cover and simmer very gently for about 1 hour, until tender and no free liquid remains.

3 Remove the cinnamon stick from the rice and stir in the sugar and orange rind.

4 Tip the fruit into the base of a lightly oiled 1.5 litre/2½ pint/6¼ cup ring mould. Spoon the rice over, smoothing down firmly. Chill until needed.

5 Run a knife around the edge of the mould and turn out the rice carefully on to a serving plate.

Cherry Pancakes

These pancakes are virtually fat-free, and lower in calories and higher in fibre than traditional ones. Serve with natural yogurt.

INGREDIENTS

Serves 4

50g/2oz/½ cup plain (all-purpose) flour
50g/2oz/½ cup wholemeal (whole-wheat) flour
pinch of salt
1 egg white
150ml/¼ pint/⅔ cup skimmed milk
a little oil for frying

For the filling
425g/15oz can black cherries in juice
7.5ml/1½ tsp arrowroot

1 Sift the flours and salt into a bowl, adding any bran left in the sieve to the bowl at the end.

2 Make a well in the centre of the flour and add the egg white. Gradually beat in the milk and 150ml/¼ pint/⅔ cup of water, whisking hard until all the liquid is incorporated and the batter is smooth and bubbly.

3 Heat a non-stick frying pan with a small amount of oil until the pan is very hot. Pour in just enough batter to cover the bottom of the pan, swirling the pan to cover the base evenly.

4 Cook until the pancake is set and golden, and then turn to cook the other side. Remove to a sheet of absorbent paper and then cook the remaining batter to make about eight pancakes.

5 Drain the cherries, reserving the juice. Blend about 30ml/2 tbsp of the juice from the can of cherries with the arrowroot in a pan. Stir in the rest of the juice. Heat gently, stirring, until boiling. Stir over a moderate heat for about 2 minutes, until thickened and clear.

6 Add the cherries and stir until thoroughly heated. Spoon the cherries into the pancakes and fold them into quarters.

COOK'S TIP

The basic pancakes will freeze very successfully. Interleave them with non-stick (waxed) paper, wrap them in polythene (plastic) and seal. Freeze for up to six months. Thaw at room temperature.

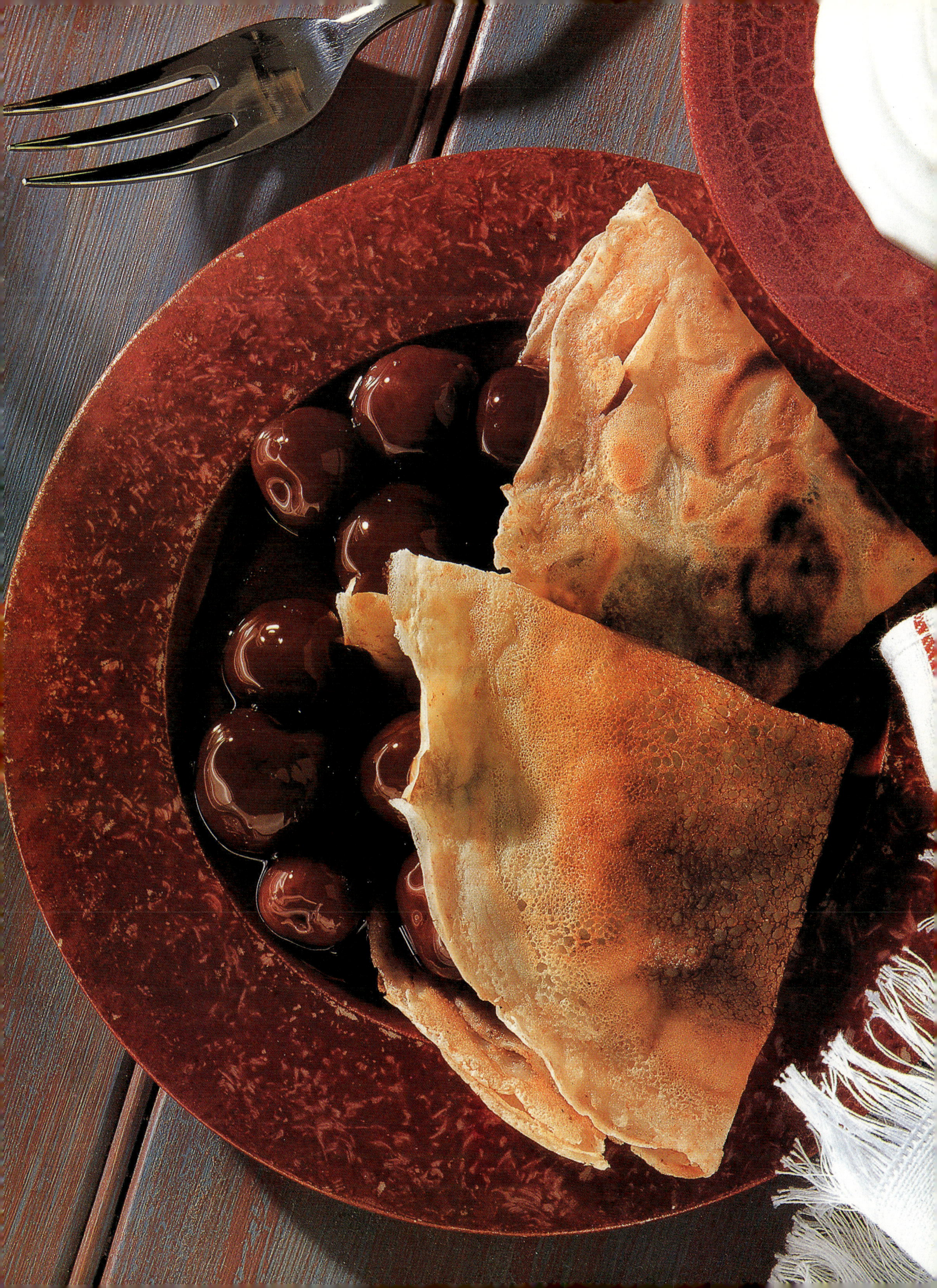

Chocolate Vanilla Timbales

A chocolate treat to enjoy with a clear conscience!

INGREDIENTS

Serves 6

350ml/12fl oz/1½ cups semi-skimmed (low-fat) milk
30ml/2 tbsp cocoa powder
2 eggs
5ml/1 tsp vanilla essence (extract)
45ml/3 tbsp caster (superfine) sugar
15ml/1 tbsp/1 sachet powdered gelatine, or alternative
sprig of mint, to decorate

For the sauce
115g/4oz/½ cup light Greek (strained, plain) yogurt
2.5ml/½ tsp vanilla essence
extra cocoa powder, to sprinkle

1 Place the milk and cocoa in a saucepan and stir until the milk is boiling. Separate the eggs and beat the egg yolks with the vanilla and sugar in a bowl, until the mixture is pale and smooth. Gradually pour in the chocolate milk, beating well.

2 Return the mixture to the pan and stir constantly over a gentle heat, without boiling, until it's slightly thickened and smooth. Dissolve the gelatine in 45ml/ 3 tbsp of hot water and then quickly stir it into the milk mixture. Let it cool until it's on the point of setting.

3 Whisk the egg whites until they hold soft peaks. Fold the egg whites quickly into the milk mixture. Spoon the timbale mixture into six individual moulds and chill them until set.

4 To serve, run a knife around the edge, dip the moulds quickly into hot water and turn out the chocolate timbales on to serving plates and decorate with a sprig of mint. For the sauce, stir together the yogurt and vanilla, spoon on to the plates and sprinkle with a little more cocoa powder.

Grilled Nectarines with Ricotta and Spice

This easy dessert is good at any time of year.

INGREDIENTS

Serves 4

4 ripe nectarines or peaches

15ml/1 tbsp light muscovado (molasses) sugar

115g/4oz/½ cup ricotta cheese or fromage frais

2.5ml/½ tsp ground star anise

1 Cut the nectarines in half and remove the stones (pits).

2 Arrange the nectarines, cut-side upwards, in a wide flameproof dish or on a baking sheet.

3 Stir the sugar into the ricotta or fromage frais. Using a teaspoon, spoon the mixture into the hollow of each nectarine half.

4 Sprinkle with the star anise. Place under a moderately hot grill (broiler) for 6–8 minutes, or until the nectarines are hot and bubbling. Serve warm.

COOK'S TIP

Star anise has a deliciously warm, rich flavour – if you can't get it, try ground cloves instead.

Crunchy Gooseberry Crumble

Gooseberries are perfect for traditional family puddings like this one. When they are out of season, other fruits such as apples, plums or rhubarb could be used instead.

INGREDIENTS

Serves 4

500g/1¼lb/5 cups gooseberries
50g/2oz/4 tbsp caster (superfine) sugar
75g/3oz/scant 1 cup rolled oats
75g/3oz/⅔ cup wholemeal (whole-wheat) flour
60ml/4 tbsp sunflower oil
50g/2oz/4 tbsp demerara (raw) sugar
30ml/2 tbsp chopped walnuts
plain yogurt, to serve

1 Preheat the oven to 200°C/400°F/Gas 6. Place the gooseberries in a pan with the caster sugar. Cover the pan and cook over a low heat for 10 minutes, until the gooseberries are just tender. Tip into an ovenproof dish.

2 To make the crumble topping, place the oats, flour and oil in a bowl and stir with a fork until evenly mixed.

3 Stir in the demerara sugar and walnuts, then spread evenly over the gooseberries. Bake for 25–30 minutes, or until golden and bubbling. Serve hot with yogurt.

COOK'S TIP

The best gooseberries to use for cooking are the early, small, firm green ones.

Floating Islands in Hot Plum Sauce

A low-fat version of the French classic, that is simpler to make than it looks. The plum sauce can be made in advance, and reheated just before you cook the meringues.

INGREDIENTS

Serves 4

450g/1lb red plums
300ml/½ pint/1¼ cups apple juice
2 egg whites
30ml/2 tbsp concentrated apple juice syrup
freshly grated nutmeg, to serve

1 Halve the plums and remove the stones (pits). Place them in a wide pan, with the apple juice.

2 Bring to the boil and then cover with a lid and leave to simmer gently for 20–30 minutes or until the plums are tender.

3 Place the egg whites in a clean, dry bowl and whisk them until they hold soft peaks.

4 Gradually whisk in the apple juice syrup, whisking until the meringue holds fairly firm peaks.

5 Using a tablespoon, scoop the meringue mixture into the gently simmering plum sauce. You may need to cook the "islands" in two batches.

6 Cover and allow to simmer gently for 2–3 minutes, until the meringues are just set. Serve straight away, sprinkled with a little freshly grated nutmeg.

COOK'S TIP

A bottle of concentrated apple juice is a useful store cupboard sweetener, but if you don't have any, use a little honey instead.

Cakes and Gâteaux

Devil's Food Cake with Orange Frosting

Chocolate and orange are the ultimate combination. Can you resist the temptation?

INGREDIENTS

Serves 8–10

50g/2oz/½ cup unsweetened cocoa powder
175g/6oz/¾ cup butter, at room temperature
350g/12oz/1½ cups soft dark brown sugar, firmly packed
3 eggs, at room temperature
225g/8oz/2 cups plain (all-purpose) flour
25ml/1½ tsp baking soda
1.5ml/¼ tsp baking powder
175ml/6fl oz/¾ cup sour cream
orange rind strips, for decoration

For the frosting
285g/10½oz/1½ cups granulated sugar
2 egg whites
60ml/4 tbsp frozen orange juice concentrate
15ml/1 tbsp fresh lemon juice
grated rind of 1 orange

1 Preheat the oven to 180°C/350°F/Gas 4. Line two 23cm/9in cake tins (pans) with greaseproof (waxed) paper, and grease. In a bowl, mix the cocoa and 175ml/6fl oz/¾ cup of boiling water until smooth. Set aside.

2 With an electric mixer, cream the butter and sugar until light and fluffy. Add the eggs, one at a time, beating well.

3 When the cocoa mixture is lukewarm, stir into the butter mixture.

4 Sift together the flour, baking soda and baking powder twice. Fold into the cocoa mixture in three batches, alternating with the sour cream.

5 Pour into the tins. Bake until the cakes pull away from the tin, 30–35 minutes. Stand for 15 minutes before unmoulding.

6 Thinly slice the orange rind strips. Blanch in boiling water for 1 minute.

7 For the frosting, place all the ingredients in the top of a double boiler or in a bowl set over hot water. With an electric mixer, beat until the mixture holds soft peaks. Continue beating off the heat until thick enough to spread.

8 Sandwich the cake with frosting, then spread over the top and sides. Arrange the rind on top.

Angel Cake

This cake is beautifully light. The secret? Sifting the flour over and over again to let plenty of air into it.

INGREDIENTS

Serves 12–14

115g/4oz/1 cup sifted cake flour
285g/10½oz/1½ cups caster (superfine) sugar
300ml/½ pint/1¼ cups egg whites (about 10–11 eggs)
6.5ml/1¼ tsp cream of tartar
1.5ml/¼ tsp salt
5ml/1 tsp vanilla essence (extract)
1.5ml/¼ tsp almond essence (extract)
icing (confectioners') sugar, for dusting

1 Preheat the oven to 160°C/325°F/Gas 3. Sift the flour before measuring, then sift it four times with 90g/3½oz/½ cup of the sugar. Transfer to a bowl.

2 With an electric mixer, beat the egg whites until foamy. Sift over the cream of tartar and salt and continue to beat until they hold soft peaks when the beaters are lifted.

3 Add the remaining sugar in three batches, beating well after each addition. Stir in the vanilla and almond essence.

4 Add the flour mixture, ½ cup at a time, and fold in gently with a large metal spoon after each addition.

5 Transfer to an ungreased 25cm/10in straight-sided ring mould and bake until delicately browned on top, about 1 hour.

6 Turn the ring mould upside down on to a cake rack and let cool for 1 hour. If the cake does not unmould, run a spatula around the edge to loosen it. When cook, transfer to a serving plate.

7 Lay a star-shaped template on top of the cake, sift icing sugar over, and lift off.

Cakes and Gâteaux • 77

Black Forest Gâteau

This light chocolate sponge, moistened with Kirsch and layered with cherries and cream, is still one of the most popular of all the chocolate gâteaux.

INGREDIENTS

Serves 8–10

6 eggs

200g/7oz/scant 1 cup caster (superfine) sugar

5ml/1 tsp vanilla essence (extract)

50g/2oz/½ cup plain (all-purpose) flour

50g/2oz/½ cup cocoa powder

115g/4oz/½ cup unsalted butter, melted

For the filling and topping

60ml/4 tbsp Kirsch

600ml/1 pint/2½ cups double (heavy) or whipping cream

30ml/2 tbsp icing (confectioners') sugar

2.5ml/½ tsp vanilla essence

675g/1½lb jar pitted morello (red) cherries, drained

To decorate

icing sugar, for dusting

grated chocolate

chocolate curls

fresh or drained canned morello cherries

1 Preheat the oven to 180°C/350°F/Gas 4. Grease three 19cm/7½in sandwich cake tins (pans) and line the base of each with baking parchment. Whisk the eggs with the sugar and vanilla essence in a large bowl until pale and very thick – the mixture should hold a firm trail when the whisk is lifted.

2 Sift the flour and cocoa over the mixture and fold in lightly and evenly. Stir in the melted butter. Divide the mixture among the prepared cake tins, smoothing them level.

3 Bake for 15–18 minutes, until risen and springy to the touch. Leave to cool in the tins for about 5 minutes, then turn out on to wire racks and leave to cool completely.

4 Prick each layer all over with a skewer or fork, then sprinkle with Kirsch. Whip the cream in a bowl until it starts to thicken, then beat in the icing sugar and vanilla essence until the mixture begins to hold its shape.

5 To assemble, spread one cake layer with a thick layer of flavoured cream and top with a quarter of the cherries. Spread a second cake layer with cream and cherries, then place it on top of the first layer. Top with the final layer.

6 Spread the remaining cream all over the cake. Dust a plate with icing sugar; position the cake. Press grated chocolate over the sides and decorate with the chocolate curls and cherries.

Raspberry Meringue Gâteau

A rich, hazelnut meringue sandwiched with whipped cream and raspberries makes an irresistible dessert for a special occasion.

INGREDIENTS

Serves 6

4 egg whites
225g/8oz/1 cup caster (superfine) sugar
a few drops of vanilla essence (extract)
5ml/1 tsp distilled malt vinegar
115g/4oz/1 cup roasted and chopped hazelnuts, ground
300ml/½ pint/1¼ cups double (heavy) cream
350g/12oz/2 cups raspberries
icing (confectioners') sugar, for dusting
mint sprigs, to decorate

For the sauce

225g/8oz/1⅓ cups raspberries
45–60ml/3–4 tbsp icing sugar, sifted
15ml/1 tbsp orange liqueur

1 Preheat the oven to 180°C/350°F/Gas 4. Grease two 20cm/8in sandwich tins (pans) and line the bases with greaseproof (waxed) paper.

2 Whisk the egg whites in a large bowl until they hold stiff peaks, then gradually whisk in the caster sugar a tablespoon at a time, whisking well after each addition.

3 Continue whisking the meringue mixture for a minute of two until very stiff, then fold in the vanilla essence, vinegar and ground hazelnuts.

4 Divide the meringue mixture between the prepared sandwich tins and spread level. Bake for 50–60 minutes, until crisp. Remove the meringues from the tins and leave them to cool on a wire rack.

5 While the meringues are cooling, make the sauce. Process the raspberries with the icing sugar and orange liqueur in a blender or food processor, then press the purée through a fine sieve to remove any pips. Chill the sauce until ready to serve.

6 Whip the cream until it forms soft peaks, then gently fold in the raspberries. Sandwich the meringue rounds together with the raspberry cream.

7 Dust the top of the gâteau with icing sugar. Decorate with mint sprigs and serve with the raspberry sauce.

VARIATION

Fresh redcurrants make a good alternative to raspberries. Pick over the fruit, then pull each sprig gently through the prongs of a fork to release the redcurrants. Add them to the whipped cream with a little icing sugar, to taste.

COOK'S TIP

You can buy roasted chopped hazelnuts in supermarkets. Otherwise toast whole hazelnuts under the grill (broiler) and rub off the flaky skins using a clean dish towel. To chop finely, process in a blender or food processor for a few moments.

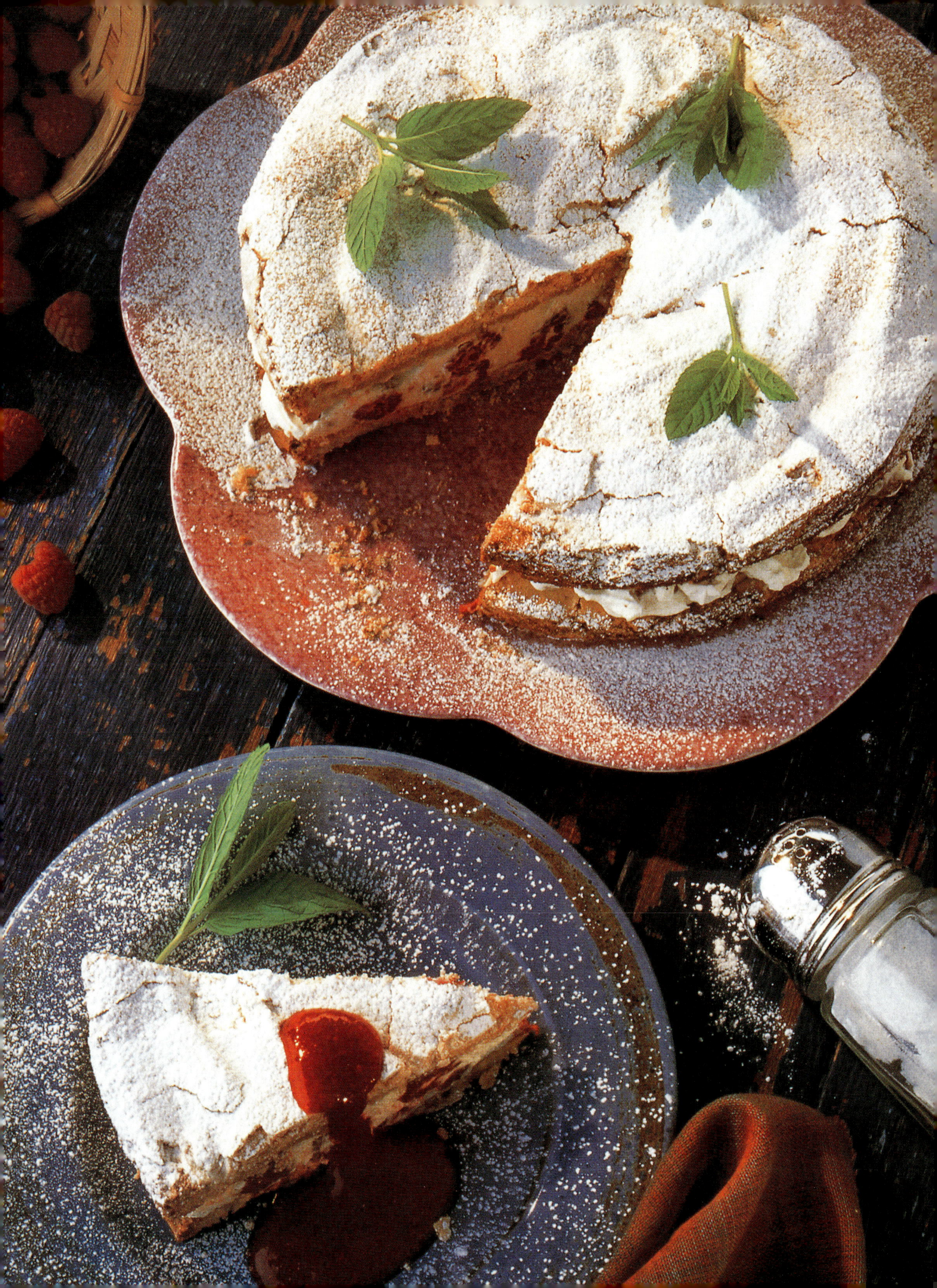

Chocolate Mousse Strawberry Layer Cake

The strawberries can be replaced by raspberries or blackberries and the appropriate flavour liqueur.

INGREDIENTS

Serves 10

115g/4oz fine quality white chocolate, chopped
120ml/4fl oz/½ cup whipping or double (heavy) cream
120ml/4fl oz/½ cup milk
15ml/1 tbsp rum or vanilla essence (extract)
115g/4oz/½ cup unsalted butter, softened
175g/6oz/generous ¾ cup granulated sugar
3 eggs
275g/10oz/2½ cups plain (all-purpose) flour
5ml/1 tsp baking powder
pinch of salt
675g/1½lb fresh strawberries, sliced, plus extra for decoration
750ml/1¼ pints/3 cups whipping cream
30ml/2 tbsp rum or strawberry-flavour liqueur

For the white chocolate mousse
250g/9oz fine quality white chocolate, chopped
350ml/12fl oz/1½ cups whipping or double (heavy) cream
30ml/2 tbsp rum or strawberry-flavour liqueur

1 Preheat the oven to 180°C/350°F/ Gas 4. Grease and flour two 23 x 5cm/9 x 2in cake tins (pans). Line the bases of the tins with baking parchment. Melt the chocolate and cream in a double boiler over a low heat, stirring until smooth. Stir in the milk and rum or vanilla essence; set aside to cool.

2 In a large bowl with an electric mixer, beat the butter and sugar until light and creamy. Add the eggs one at a time, beating well.

3 In a small bowl, stir together the flour, baking powder and salt. Alternately add flour and melted chocolate to the eggs in batches, until just blended. Pour the batter evenly into the tins.

4 Bake for 20–25 minutes until a cake tester inserted in the centre comes out clean. Cool on a wire rack for 10 minutes. Turn the cakes out on to a wire rack, peel off the paper and cool completely.

5 Prepare the mousse. In a medium pan over low heat, melt the chocolate and cream until smooth, stirring frequently. Stir in the rum or strawberry-flavour liqueur and pour into a bowl. Chill until just set. With a wire whisk, whip lightly until the mixture has a "mousse" consistency.

6 Slice both cake layers in half crossways. Sandwich the four layers together with the mousse and strawberries.

7 Whip the cream with the rum or liqueur until firm peaks form. Spread half over the top and sides of the cake. Spoon the remaining cream into a piping (icing) bag with a star tip and pipe scrolls on top. Decorate with strawberries.

Death by Chocolate

One of the richest chocolate cakes ever, so serve in thin slices.

INGREDIENTS

Serves 16–20

225g/8oz plain (semisweet) chocolate, broken into squares
115g/4oz/½ cup unsalted butter
150ml/¼ pint/⅔ cup milk
225g/8oz/1¼ cups soft light brown sugar
10ml/2 tsp vanilla essence (extract)
2 eggs, separated
150ml/¼ pint/⅔ cup sour cream
225g/8oz/2 cups self-raising flour
5ml/1 tsp baking powder

For the filling
60ml/4 tbsp seedless raspberry jam
60ml/4 tbsp brandy
400g/14oz plain chocolate, broken into squares
200g/7oz/scant 1 cup unsalted butter

For the (chocolate) ganache topping
250ml/8fl oz/1 cup double (heavy) cream
225g/8oz plain (semisweet) chocolate, broken into squares
plain and white chocolate curls, to decorate
chocolate-dipped Cape gooseberries, to serve (optional)

1 Preheat the oven to 180°C/350°F/Gas 4. Grease and base-line a deep 23cm/9in springform cake tin (pan). Place the chocolate, butter and milk in a pan. Heat gently until smooth. Remove from the heat, beat in the sugar and vanilla, then cool.

2 Beat the egg yolks and cream in a bowl, then beat into the chocolate mixture. Sift the flour and baking powder over the surface and fold in. Whisk the egg whites in a grease-free bowl until stiff; fold into the mixture.

3 Scrape into the prepared tin and bake for 45–55 minutes, or until firm to the touch. Cool in the tin for 15 minutes, then invert to a wire rack to cool.

4 Slice the cold cake across the middle to make three even layers. In a small pan, warm the jam with 15ml/1 tbsp of the brandy, then brush over two of the layers. Heat the remaining brandy in a pan with the chocolate and butter, stirring, until smooth. Cool until beginning to thicken.

5 Spread the bottom layer of the cake with half the chocolate filling, taking care not to disturb the jam. Top with a second layer, jam side up, and spread with the remaining filling. Top with the final layer and press lightly. Leave to set.

6 To make the topping, heat the cream and chocolate together in a pan over a low heat, stirring frequently until the chocolate has melted. Pour into a bowl, leave to cool, then whisk until the mixture begins to hold its shape.

7 Spread the top and sides of the cake with the chocolate ganache. Decorate with chocolate curls and, if liked, chocolate-dipped Cape gooseberries.

Simple Chocolate Cake

An easy, everyday chocolate cake which can be filled with buttercream, or with a rich chocolate ganache for a special occasion.

INGREDIENTS

Serves 6–8

115g/4oz plain (semisweet) chocolate, broken into squares

45ml/3 tbsp milk

150g/5oz/⅔ cup unsalted butter or margarine, softened

150g/5oz/scant 1 cup soft light brown sugar

3 eggs

200g/7oz/1¾ cups self-raising (self-rising) flour

15ml/1 tbsp cocoa powder

For the buttercream

75g/3oz/6 tbsp unsalted butter or margarine, softened

175g/6oz/1½ cups icing (confectioners') sugar

15ml/1 tbsp cocoa powder

2.5ml/½ tsp vanilla essence (extract)

icing sugar and cocoa powder, for dusting

1 Preheat the oven to 180°C/350°F/Gas 4. Grease two 18cm/7in round sandwich cake tins (pans) and line the base of each with baking parchment. Melt the chocolate with the milk in a heatproof bowl set over a pan of simmering water.

2 Cream the butter or margarine with the sugar in a mixing bowl until pale and fluffy. Add the eggs one at a time, beating well after each addition. Stir in the chocolate mixture until it is well combined.

3 Sift the flour and cocoa over the mixture and fold in with a metal spoon until evenly mixed. Scrape into the prepared tins, smooth level and bake for 35–40 minutes or until well risen and firm. Turn out on wire racks and leave to cool.

4 To make the buttercream, beat the butter or margarine, icing sugar, cocoa powder and vanilla essence together in a bowl until the mixture is smooth.

5 Sandwich the cake layers together with the buttercream. Dust with a mixture of icing sugar and cocoa just before serving.

Sachertorte

This glorious gâteau was created in Vienna in 1832 by Franz Sacher, a chef in the royal household.

INGREDIENTS

Serves 10–12

225g/8oz plain (semisweet) dark chocolate, broken into squares
150g/5oz/⅔ cup unsalted butter, softened
115g/4oz/generous ½ cup caster (superfine) sugar
8 eggs, separated
115g/4oz/1 cup plain (all-purpose) flour

For the glaze
225g/8oz/scant 1 cup apricot jam
15ml/1 tbsp lemon juice

For the icing
225g/8oz plain dark chocolate, broken into squares
200g/7oz/1 cup caster sugar
15ml/1 tbsp golden (light corn) syrup
250ml/8fl oz/1 cup double (heavy) cream
5ml/1 tsp vanilla essence (extract)
plain chocolate curls, to decorate

1 Preheat the oven to 180°C/350°F/Gas 4. Grease a 23cm/9in round springform cake tin (pan) and line with baking parchment. Melt the chocolate in a heatproof bowl over hot water, then remove from the heat.

2 Cream the butter with the sugar in a mixing bowl until pale and fluffy, then add the egg yolks, one at a time, beating after each addition. Beat in the melted chocolate, then sift the flour over the mixture and fold it in evenly.

3 Whisk the egg whites in a clean, grease-free bowl until stiff, then stir about a quarter of the whites into the chocolate mixture to lighten it. Fold in the remaining whites.

4 Tip the mixture into the prepared cake tin and smooth level. Bake for about 50–55 minutes, or until firm. Turn out carefully on to a wire rack to cool.

5 Heat the apricot jam with the lemon juice in a small pan until melted, then strain through a sieve into a bowl. Once the cake is cold, slice in half across the middle to make two equal-size layers.

6 Brush the top and sides of each layer with the apricot glaze, then sandwich them together. Place on a wire rack.

7 Mix the icing ingredients in a heavy pan. Heat gently, stirring until thick. Simmer for 3–4 minutes, without stirring, until the mixture registers 95°C/200°F on a sugar thermometer. Pour quickly over the cake and spread evenly. Leave to set, then decorate with chocolate curls.

TARTS AND PIES

Red Berry Tart with Lemon Cream Filling

This flan is best filled just before serving so the pastry remains mouth-wateringly crisp.

INGREDIENTS

Serves 6–8

150g/5oz/1¼ cups plain (all-purpose) flour
25g/1oz/¼ cup cornflour (cornstarch)
40g/1½oz/5 tbsp icing (confectioners') sugar
90g/3½oz/7 tbsp butter
5ml/1 tsp vanilla essence (extract)
2 egg yolks, beaten
sprig of mint, to decorate

For the filling
200g/7oz/scant 1 cup cream cheese
45ml/3 tbsp lemon curd
grated rind and juice of 1 lemon
icing sugar, to sweeten (optional)
225g/8oz/2 cups mixed red berry fruits
45ml/3 tbsp redcurrant jelly

1 Sift the flour, cornflour and icing sugar together, then rub in the butter until the mixture resembles breadcrumbs.

2 Beat the vanilla into the egg yolks, then mix into the crumbs to make a firm dough, adding a little cold water if necessary.

3 Roll out and line a 23cm/9in round flan tin (pan), trim and press the dough up the sides. Prick the base with a fork and rest it in the refrigerator for 30 minutes.

4 Preheat the oven to 200°C/400°F/Gas 6. Line the flan with baking parchment and fill with baking beans. Place the tin on a baking sheet and bake for 20 minutes, removing the paper and beans for the last 5 minutes. When cooked, cool and remove the pastry case from the flan tin.

5 Cream the cheese, lemon curd and lemon rind and juice, adding icing sugar to sweeten, if you wish. Spread the mixture into the base of the flan.

6 Top the flan with the fruits. Gently warm the redcurrant jelly and trickle it over the fruits just before serving the flan decorated with a sprig of mint.

VARIATION

This recipe works equally well for individual tartlets, and there are all sorts of delightful variations. For instance, leave out the redcurrant jelly and sprinkle lightly with icing sugar or decorate with fresh strawberry leaves.

Raspberry Tart

This glazed fruit tart really does taste as good as it looks.

INGREDIENTS

Serves 8

4 egg yolks
65g/2½ oz/⅓ cup granulated sugar
45ml/3 tbsp plain (all-purpose) flour
300ml/½ pint/1¼ cups milk
pinch of salt
2.5ml/½ tsp vanilla essence (extract)
450g/1lb fresh raspberries
75ml/5 tbsp grape or redcurrant jelly
15ml/1 tbsp fresh orange juice

For the pastry
150g/5oz/1¼ cups plain flour
2.5ml/½ tsp baking powder
1.5ml/¼ tsp salt
15ml/1 tbsp sugar
grated rind of ½ orange
90ml/6 tbsp cold butter, cut in pieces
1 egg yolk
45–60ml/3–4 tbsp whipping cream

1 For the pastry, sift the flour, baking powder and salt into a bowl. Stir in the sugar and orange rind. Rub in the butter until the mixture resembles coarse crumbs. With a fork, stir in the egg yolk and just enough cream to bind the dough. Make into a ball, wrap in greaseproof (waxed) paper and chill.

2 For the custard filling, beat the egg yolks and sugar until thick and lemon-coloured. Gradually stir in the flour.

3 In a pan, bring the milk and salt just to the boil, and remove from the heat. Whisk into the egg yolk mixture, return to the pan, and continue whisking over moderately high heat until just bubbling. Cook for 3 minutes to thicken. Transfer immediately to a bowl. Stir in the vanilla to blend.

4 Cover with greaseproof paper to prevent a skin from forming.

5 Preheat the oven to 200°C/ 400°F/Gas 6. On a lightly floured surface, roll out the dough about 3mm/⅛in thick, transfer to a 25cm/10in flan tin (pan) and trim the edge. Prick the bottom all over with a fork and line with greaseproof paper. Fill with baking beans and bake for 15 minutes. Remove the paper and baking beans. Continue baking until golden, 6–8 minutes more. Let cool.

6 Spread an even layer of the pastry cream filling in the tart shell and arrange the raspberries on top. Melt the jelly and orange juice in a pan over a low heat and brush on top to glaze.

Kiwi Ricotta Cheese Tart

It is well worth taking your time arranging the kiwi fruit topping in neat rows for this exotic and impressive-looking tart.

INGREDIENTS

Serves 8

50g/2oz/½ cup blanched almonds
90g/3½oz/½ cup plus 15ml/1 tbsp caster (superfine) sugar
900g/2lb/4 cups ricotta cheese
250ml/8fl oz/1 cup whipping cream
1 egg
3 egg yolks
15ml/1 tbsp plain (all-purpose) flour
pinch of salt
30ml/2 tbsp rum
grated rind of 1 lemon
40ml/2½ tbsp lemon juice
50ml/2fl oz/¼ cup clear honey
5 kiwi fruit

For the pastry
150g/5oz/1¼ cups plain flour
15ml/1 tbsp granulated sugar
2.5ml/½ tsp salt
2.5ml/½ tsp baking powder
75g/3oz/6 tbsp cold butter, cut in pieces
1 egg yolk
45–60ml/3–4 tbsp whipping cream

1 For the pastry, sift the flour, sugar, salt and baking powder into a bowl. Cut in the butter until the mixture resembles coarse crumbs. Mix the egg yolk and cream. Stir in just enough to bind the dough.

2 Transfer to a lightly floured surface, flatten slightly, wrap in greaseproof (waxed) paper and chill for 30 minutes. Preheat the oven to 220°C/425°F/Gas 7.

3 On a floured surface, roll out the dough 3mm/⅛in thick and transfer to a 23cm/9in springform tin (pan). Crimp the edge.

4 Prick the bottom of the dough all over with a fork. Line with baking parchment and fill with baking beans. Bake for 10 minutes. Remove the paper and beans and bake until golden, 6–8 minutes more. Let cool. Reduce the heat to 180°C/350°F/Gas 4.

5 Grind the almonds finely with 15ml/1 tbsp of the sugar in a food processor or blender.

6 With an electric mixer, beat the ricotta until creamy. Add the cream, egg, yolks, remaining sugar, flour, salt, rum, lemon rind and 30ml/2 tbsp of the lemon juice. Beat to combine.

7 Stir in the ground almonds until well blended.

8 Pour into the shell and bake until golden, about 1 hour. Let cool, then chill, loosely covered, for 2–3 hours. Unmould and place on a serving plate.

9 Combine the honey and remaining lemon juice for the glaze. Set aside.

10 Peel the kiwis. Halve them lengthwise, then cut crosswise into 5mm/¼in slices. Arrange the slices in rows across the top of the tart. Just before serving, brush with the glaze.

Lemon and Orange Tart

Refreshing citrus fruits in a crisp, nutty pastry case.

INGREDIENTS

Serves 8–10

115g/4oz/1 cup plain (all-purpose) flour, sifted
115g/4oz/1 cup wholemeal (whole-wheat) flour
25g/1oz/3 tbsp ground hazelnuts
25g/1oz/3 tbsp icing (confectioners') sugar, sifted
pinch of salt
115g/4oz/½ cup unsalted butter
60ml/4 tbsp lemon curd
300ml/½ pint/1¼ cups whipped cream
4 oranges, peeled and thinly sliced

1 Place the flours, hazelnuts, sugar, salt and butter in a food processor and process in short bursts until the mixture resembles breadcrumbs. Add 30–45ml/2–3 tbsp cold water and process until the dough comes together.

2 Turn out on to a lightly floured surface and knead gently until smooth. Roll out and line a 25cm/10in flan tin (pan). Ease the pastry gently into the corners without stretching it. Chill for 20 minutes. Preheat the oven to 190°C/375°F/Gas 5.

3 Line the pastry with baking parchment and fill with baking beans. Bake blind for 15 minutes, remove the paper and beans and continue for a further 5–10 minutes, until the pastry is crisp. Allow to cool.

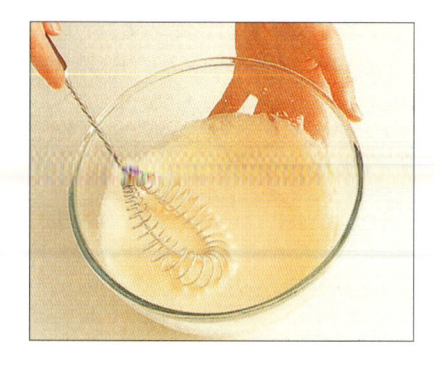

4 Whisk the lemon curd into the cream and spread over the base of the pastry. Arrange the orange slices on top and serve at room temperature.

Chocolate Pear Tart

This tart is delicious served with vanilla ice cream.

INGREDIENTS

Serves 8

115g/4oz plain (semisweet) chocolate, grated
3 large firm, ripe pears
1 egg
1 egg yolk
120ml/4fl oz/½ cup single (light) cream
2.5ml/½ tsp vanilla essence (extract)
45ml/3 tbsp caster (superfine) sugar

For the pastry

115g/4oz/1 cup plain (all-purpose) flour
pinch of salt
30ml/2 tbsp caster sugar
115g/4oz/½ cup cold unsalted butter, cut into pieces
1 egg yolk
15ml/1 tbsp fresh lemon juice

1 For the pastry, sift the flour and salt into a bowl. Add the sugar and butter. Cut in with a pastry blender until the mixture resembles coarse crumbs. With a fork, stir in the egg yolk and lemon juice until the mixture forms a dough. Gather into a ball, wrap in greaseproof (waxed) paper, and chill for at least 20 minutes.

2 Place a baking sheet in the oven and preheat to 200°C/400°F/Gas 6. On a lightly floured surface, roll out the dough to 3mm/⅛in thick and transfer to a 25cm/10in flan tin (pan). Trim the edge.

3 Sprinkle the bottom of the tart shell with the grated chocolate.

4 Peel, halve and core the pears. Cut in thin slices crosswise, then fan them out slightly.

5 Transfer the pear halves to the tart with the help of a metal spatula and arrange on top of the chocolate to resemble the spokes of a wheel.

6 Whisk together the egg and egg yolk, cream and vanilla essence. Ladle over the pears, then sprinkle with sugar.

7 Bake for 10 minutes. Reduce the heat to 180°C/350°F/Gas 4 and cook until the custard is set and the pears begin to caramelize, about 20 minutes more. Serve at room temperature.

Treacle Tart

Quite a filling tart, this, so best served after a light main course.

INGREDIENTS

Serves 4–6

175ml/6fl oz/¾ cup golden (light corn) syrup
75g/3oz/1½ cups fresh white breadcrumbs
grated rind of 1 lemon
30ml/2 tbsp fresh lemon juice

For the pastry

150g/5oz/1¼ cups plain (all-purpose) flour
2.5ml/½ tsp salt
75g/3oz/6 tbsp cold butter, cut in pieces
75g/3oz/3 tbsp cold margarine, cut in pieces

1 For the pastry, mix the flour and salt in a bowl. Cut in the fats with a pastry blender until the mixture resembles coarse crumbs.

2 With a fork, stir in just enough iced water (about 45–60ml/3–4 tbsp) to bind the dough. Gather into a ball, wrap in greaseproof (waxed) paper, and chill for at least 20 minutes.

3 On a lightly floured surface, roll out the dough 3mm/⅛in thick. Transfer to a 20cm/8in flan tin (pan) and trim off the overhang. Chill for at least 20 minutes. Reserve the trimmings for the lattice top.

4 Place a baking sheet above the centre of the oven and heat to 200°C/400°F/Gas 6.

5 In a pan, warm the syrup until thin and runny.

6 Remove from the heat and stir in the breadcrumbs and lemon rind. Let sit for 10 minutes so the bread can absorb the syrup. Add more breadcrumbs if the mixture is thin. Stir in the lemon juice and spread evenly in the pastry shell.

7 Roll out the pastry trimmings and cut into 10–12 thin strips.

8 Lay half the strips on the filling, then carefully arrange the remaining strips to form a lattice pattern.

9 Place on the hot sheet and bake for 10 minutes. Lower the heat to 190°C/375°F/Gas 5. Bake until golden, about 15 minutes more. Serve warm or cold.

Bakewell Tart

A classic English dessert named after the town from whence it came.

INGREDIENTS

Serves 4

225g/8oz ready-made puff pastry
30ml/2 tbsp raspberry or apricot jam
2 eggs
2 egg yolks
115g/4oz/generous ½ cup caster (superfine) sugar
115g/4oz/½ cup butter, melted
50g/2oz/½ cup ground almonds
few drops of almond essence (extract)
icing (confectioners') sugar, for sifting

1 Preheat the oven to 200°C/400°F/Gas 6. Roll out the pastry on a lightly floured surface and use it to line an 18cm/7in pie plate or loose-based flan tin (pan). Spread the jam over the bottom of the pastry case.

2 Whisk the eggs, egg yolks and sugar together in a large bowl until thick and pale.

3 Gently stir the butter, ground almonds and almond essence into the mixture.

4 Pour the mixture into the pastry case and bake for 30 minutes, until the filling is just set and browned. Sift icing sugar over the top before serving the tart hot, warm or cold.

VARIATION

Ground hazelnuts are increasingly available and make an interesting change to the almonds in this tart. If you are going to grind shelled hazelnuts yourself, first roast them in the oven for 10–15 minutes to bring out their flavour, then rub in a dish towel to remove the skins.

COOK'S TIP

Since this pastry case isn't baked blind first, place a baking sheet in the oven while it preheats, then place the flan tin on the hot sheet. This will ensure that the bottom of the pastry case cooks right through.

Apple Pie

Delicious on its own, or with cream or vanilla ice cream.

INGREDIENTS

Serves 8

900g/2lb tart cooking apples
30ml/2 tbsp plain (all-purpose) flour
90g/3½oz/½ cup sugar
25ml/1½ tbsp fresh lemon juice
2.5ml/½ tsp ground cinnamon
2.5ml/½ tsp ground allspice
1.5ml/¼ tsp ground ginger
1.5ml/¼ tsp grated nutmeg
1.5ml/¼ tsp salt
50g/2oz/4 tbsp butter, diced

For the pastry
225g/8oz/2 cups plain flour
5ml/1 tsp salt
75g/3oz/6 tbsp cold butter, cut in pieces
50g/2oz/4 tbsp lard (shortening), cut in pieces

1 For the pastry, sift the flour and salt into a bowl.

2 Add the butter and lard and cut in with a pastry blender or rub between your fingertips until the mixture resembles coarse crumbs. With a fork, stir in just enough iced water to bind the dough (60–120ml/4–8 tbsp).

3 Gather into two balls, wrap in greaseproof (waxed) paper and chill for 20 minutes.

4 On a lightly floured surface, roll out one dough ball to 3mm/⅛in thick. Transfer to a 23cm/9in pie tin (pan) and trim the edge. Place a baking sheet in the centre of the oven and preheat to 220°C/425°F/Gas 7.

5 Peel, core and slice the apples into a bowl. Toss with the flour, sugar, lemon juice, spices and salt. Spoon into the pie shell, and dot with the butter.

6 Roll out the remaining dough. Place on top of the pie and trim to leave a 2cm/¾in overhang. Fold the overhang under the bottom dough and press to seal. Crimp the edge.

7 Roll out the scraps and cut out leaf shapes and roll balls for the decoration. Arrange on top of the pie. Cut steam vents.

8 Bake for 10 minutes. Reduce the heat to 180°C/350°F/Gas 4 and bake until golden, 40–45 minutes more. If the pie browns too quickly, protect with foil.

Mississippi Pecan Pie

This fabulous dessert started life in the United States but has become an international favourite.

INGREDIENTS

Serves 6–8

For the pastry
115g/4oz/1 cup plain (all-purpose) flour
50g/2oz/4 tbsp butter, cubed
25g/1oz/2 tbsp caster (superfine) sugar
1 egg yolk

For the filling
175g/6oz/½ cup golden (light corn) syrup
50g/2oz/⅓ cup soft dark brown sugar
50g/2oz/4 tbsp butter
3 eggs, lightly beaten
2.5ml/½ tsp vanilla essence (extract)
150g/5oz/1¼ cups pecan nuts
fresh cream or ice cream, to serve

1 Place the flour in a bowl and add the butter. Rub in the butter with your fingertips until the mixture resembles breadcrumbs, then stir in the sugar, egg yolk and about 30ml/2 tbsp cold water. Mix to a dough and knead lightly on a floured surface until smooth.

2 Roll out the pastry and use to line a 20cm/8in loose-based fluted flan tin (pan). Prick the base, then line with baking parchment and fill with baking beans. Chill for 30 minutes. Preheat the oven to 200°C/400°F/Gas 6.

3 Bake the pastry case for 10 minutes. Remove the paper and beans and bake for 5 minutes. Reduce the oven temperature to 180°C/350°F/Gas 4.

4 Meanwhile, heat the syrup, sugar and butter in a pan until the sugar dissolves. Remove from the heat and cool slightly. Whisk in the eggs and vanilla essence and stir in the pecans.

5 Pour into the pastry case and bake for 35–40 minutes, until the filling is set. Serve with cream or ice cream.

Boston Banoffee Pie

There are many variations of this American treat; this one is easy to make and tastes wonderful.

INGREDIENTS

Serves 6–8

150g/5oz/1¼ cups plain (all-purpose) flour
225g/8oz/1 cup butter
50g/2oz/4 tbsp caster (superfine) sugar
½ x 405g/14oz can skimmed, sweetened condensed milk
115g/4oz/⅔ cup soft light brown sugar
30ml/2 tbsp golden (light corn) syrup
2 small bananas, sliced
a little lemon juice
whipped cream, and 5ml/1 tsp grated plain (semisweet) chocolate, to decorate

1 Preheat the oven to 160°C/325°F/Gas 3. Place the flour and 115g/4oz/½ cup of the butter in a food processor and blend until crumbed (or rub in with your fingertips). Stir in the caster sugar.

2 Squeeze the mixture together until it forms a dough. Press into the base of a 20cm/8in loose-based fluted flan tin (pan). Bake for 25–30 minutes.

3 Place the remaining 115g/4oz/½ cup of butter with the condensed milk, brown sugar and golden syrup in a large non-stick pan and heat gently, stirring, until the butter has melted and the sugar has dissolved.

4 Bring to a gentle boil and cook for 7 minutes, stirring all the time (to prevent burning), until the mixture thickens and turns a light caramel colour. Pour on to the cooked pastry base and leave until cold.

5 Sprinkle the bananas with lemon juice and arrange in overlapping circles on top of the caramel filling, leaving a gap in the centre. Pipe a swirl of whipped cream in the centre and sprinkle with the grated chocolate.

Index

American spiced pumpkin pie, 49
angel cake, 76
apples: apple brown Betty, 46
   apple pie, 92
   apple soufflé omelette, 44
   baked apples with apricot filling, 43
   Eve's pudding, 50
apricots: apricot and pear filo roulade, 48
   apricots with orange cream, 30
   baked apples with apricot filling, 43
   quick apricot blender whip, 61
   yogurt with apricots and pistachios, 58
Australian hazelnut pavlova, 27

baked apples with apricot filling, 43
Bakewell tart, 91
bananas: almost instant banana pudding, 62
   Brazilian coffee bananas, 65
   Boston banoffee pie, 95
   chocolate fudge sundaes, 64
Black Forest gâteau, 77
blackberries: blackberry cobbler, 45
   lemon soufflé with blackberry sauce, 29
blackcurrant sorbet, 28
Boston banoffee pie, 95
bread pudding with pecan nuts, 55
butterscotch sauce, 14
brandy butter, 14

Cabinet pudding, 50
cherries: Black Forest gâteau, 77
   cherry pancakes, 68
chocolate: Black Forest gâteau, 77
   chocolate cheesecake, 24
   chocolate fudge sauce, 15
   chocolate fudge sundaes, 64
   chocolate mandarin trifle, 18
   chocolate mousse strawberry layer cake, 80
   chocolate pear tart, 89
   chocolate profiteroles, 26
   chocolate soufflé crêpes, 42
   chocolate vanilla timbales, 70
   death by chocolate, 81
   devil's food cake with orange frosting, 75
   double chocolate snowball, 17
   glossy chocolate sauce, 15
   hot chocolate zabaglione, 40
   magic chocolate mud pudding, 39
   pears in chocolate fudge blankets, 41
   raspberry and white chocolate cheesecake, 23
   sachertorte, 83
   simple chocolate cake, 82
   white chocolate mousse with dark sauce, 22
Christmas pudding, 52
cheesecakes: chocolate, 24
   classic, 24
   kiwi ricotta cheese tart, 87
   raspberry and white chocolate, 23
coconut: white chocolate parfait, 20
coffee: Brazilian coffee bananas, 65
   chocolate fudge sundaes, 64

mocha cream pots, 35
coulis, redcurrant and raspberry, 12
crème anglaise, 13
crème brûlée, 36
crème caramel, 37
crêpes, chocolate soufflé, 42
crunchy gooseberry crumble, 72

death by chocolate, 81
devil's food cake with orange frosting, 75
double chocolate snowball, 17

Eve's pudding, 50

floating islands in hot plum sauce, 73
frudités with honey dip, 57

fruited rice ring, 67

gelatine, 12
ginger: almost instant banana pudding, 62
   ginger and orange crème brûlée, 62
gooseberry crumble, crunchy, 72
grilled nectarines with ricotta and spice, 71

honey: frudités with honey dip, 57
hot chocolate zabaglione, 40

iced praline torte, 32
Indian ice cream, 34

kiwi ricotta cheese tart, 87

lemons: lemon and orange tart, 88
   lemon soufflé with blackberry sauce, 29
   red berry tart with lemon cream filling, 85

magic chocolate mud pudding, 39
meringue: Australian hazelnut pavlova, 27
   floating islands in hot plum sauce, 73
   raspberry meringue gâteau, 78
   Mississippi pecan pie, 94
mocha cream pots, 35

nectarines, grilled with ricotta and spice, 71

oranges: apricots with orange cream, 30
   devil's food cake with orange frosting, 75
   lemon and orange tart, 88
   prune and orange pots, 60
   rhubarb and orange fool, 30

pancakes, cherry, 68
pastry: rolling out and lining a tin, 11
   finishing the edge, 11
   making choux pastry, 10
   making French flan pastry, 9
   making shortcrust pastry, 8
peach crumble, spiced, 47
pears: apricot and pear filo roulade, 48
   chocolate pear tart, 89
   pears in chocolate fudge blankets, 41
pecan pie, Mississippi, 94
pineapple: chocolate soufflé crêpes, 42
   fresh pineapple salad, 58
pistachios: Indian ice cream, 34
   yogurt with apricots and pistachios, 58
plums: floating islands in hot plum sauce, 73
prune and orange pots, 60
pumpkin pie, American, 49

raspberries: raspberry and white chocolate cheesecake, 23
   raspberry meringue gateau, 78
   raspberry tart, 86
   red berry tart with lemon cream filling, 85
redcurrant and raspberry coulis, 12
rhubarb and orange fool, 30

sabayon, 13
sachertorte, 83
sauces: butterscotch sauce, 14
   crème anglaise, 13
   chocolate fudge sauce, 15
   glossy chocolate sauce, 15
   redcurrant and raspberry coulis, 12
   sabayon, 13
sorbet, blackcurrant, 28
soufflés: apple soufflé omelette, 44
   lemon soufflé with blackberries, 29
spiced peach crumble, 47

tarts: Bakewell tart, 91
   chocolate pear tart, 89
   lemon and orange tart, 88
   kiwi ricotta cheese tart, 87
   raspberry tart, 86
   red berry tart with lemon cream filling, 85
   treacle tart, 90

Vermont baked maple custard, 54

yogurt: frudités with honey dip, 57
   prune and orange pots, 60
   quick apricot blender whip, 61
   yogurt with apricots and pistachios, 58

zabaglione, hot chocolate, 40